D1033024

1978

Merry Christmas
Dick —

With much Love,
&d Enjoyable Reading!
Shari

This Trifling Distinction

Books by John Gould

New England Town Meeting
Pre-natal Care for Fathers
Farmer Takes a Wife
The House That Jacob Built
And One to Grow On
Neither Hay nor Grass
Monstrous Depravity
The Parables of Peter Partout
You Should Start Sooner
Last One In
Europe on Saturday Night
The Jonesport Raffle
Twelve Grindstones
The Shag Bag
Glass Eyes by the Bottle
This Trifling Distinction

With F. Wenderoth Saunders:
The Fastest Hound Dog in the State of Maine
With Lillian Ross:
Maine Lingo

This Trifling Distinction

Reminiscences from Down East

By John Gould

Little, Brown and Company

BOSTON PETTIT TORONTO

FIRST EDITION

T 06/78

Material appearing on pages 36–41 of this book originally appeared in *The Parables of Peter Partout,* copyright © 1964 by John T. Gould. Reprinted with permission of Little, Brown and Company, Inc.

The material on pages 24–29, a study of horn elevations, originally appeared in *The Farm Quarterly,* winter issue of 1946, published by F & W Publishing Corporation, 22 East Twelfth Street, Cincinnati, and is reprinted here with permission.

LIBRARY OF CONGRESS CATALOGING IN PUBLICATION DATA

Gould, John, 1908-
    This trifling distinction.

    1. Gould, John, 1908-   — Biography.
2. Authors, American — 20th century — Biography.
3. Maine — Anecdotes, facetiae, satire, etc.
I. Title.
PS3513.0852Z475   818'.5'207   78-6232
ISBN 0-316-32175-3

Designed by Chris Benders

Published simultaneously in Canada
by Little, Brown & Company (Canada) Limited
PRINTED IN THE UNITED STATES OF AMERICA

For my Dorothy

This Trifling Distinction ...

. . . when these Ephraimites which were escaped said, Let me go over; that the men of Gilead said unto him, Art thou an Ephraimite? If he said, Nay, then said they unto him, Say now Shibboleth; and he said Sibboleth; for he could not frame to pronounce it right.

Apology

THE trifling distinction has been that I chose to live in Maine. When I became an "author" I noticed that bookstore sales of my Maine yarns did not immediately burst into profusion here in Maine, or even here in the East. After good sales in Los Angeles, Seattle, San Francisco, a book would work back this way, gaining as it came, and some time after publication one of my neighbors would say, "Hear you've got another book out!"

It is not uncommon for random cow-jockeys, auctioneers, sawmill operators, postmasters, ministers, and other Mainers to have a book out. That non-Mainers buy them is gratifying. There persists something about Maine that edifies and amuses the rest of the country. My reminiscences here are not meant to be an autobiography (a high-school boy in Greater Portland is writing my autobiography), but I would like them to convey some of the fun it has been to live and write, as I have, in the Pine Tree State.

A summercator once said to Hod Carter, "I find it interesting that nobody in Maine ever says 'yes.'"

Hod said, "Eyah." That's a Shibboleth.

He's used me, too.

(signed) *Peter Partout*
Peppermint Corner

This Trifling Distinction

1

AUTHORS was a tedious card game we children were permitted to play on Sundays, and because it wasn't any fun Mother thought it couldn't be evil. We children mastered cribbage, pinochle, poker, high-low-jack, and other wicked instruments of the devil at early ages, but on Sundays we had to play Authors. Scores were made by matching up bearded pictures of Longfellow, Browning, Bryant, Dickens, and other writers who had whiskers, causing me to believe from childhood that barbers were enemies of literature. My mother was not against cards, and in her nineties will still skunk you two games out of three if you suggest cribbage. But while her down-east casuistry frowned on playing cards on the Lord's Day, she saw nothing evil in playing with pasteboard objects that had authors on them. I hated Authors, and I was concerned to learn, precisely in 1945, that I had become an "author."

Whiskers had nothing to do with it. I had been writing for the newspapers and keeping the grocer paid. In 1932 I had brought my bride out of the horrors of Boston onto the Maine farm where my father and my grandfather had been born, and her adjustment to country life gave me many things to write about. I peddled them variously as each vignette of farm affairs matured, and Lester Markel, who was then Sunday editor of *The New York Times*, used a few in the paper's magazine. One of them caught the eye of Frances Phillips, an editor with the publishing house of William Morrow & Company, and she wrote to say she felt these pieces would make a book. When the pile was big enough, Morrow brought out *Farmer Takes a Wife*. The unsettled condition of public affairs during the war caused a lot of people to take a fancy to these quiet tales of farm life ("with roots down" was frequent in reviews) and the book stayed on the best-seller list for a long time.

But royalty payments are delayed. The book was earning money, all right, but I wasn't going to get any until the next April, so we struck into the winter on our usual farm program of make it do, use it up, and do without. We had skating and a roast of pork for Thanksgiving, good snow for yarding logs by Christmas, and January was real Maine-ish throughout. Impending wealth had not caused us to take on any up-stairs maids.

It was in January, about seed-catalog time, that I became an author. In the same mail with the Burpee book, I got this letter from a woman in Boston I'd never heard of who told me — she didn't *ask* me — to be at the Copley Plaza Hotel on such-and-such a date to speak at an "authors' luncheon." My wife, who was now naturalized and speaking the Maine lingo like a native, read the letter and said, "Lah-di-dah and oops! This calls for a necktie!"

There was a dear, sweet, and extremely efficient maiden lady at William Morrow, name of Polly Street, who was in charge of sales, promotion, and advertis-ing, and as a new and untried trotter in her stable I felt I should let her know that I had been thus honored. I wrote across the bottom of the letter *Is this in my contract?* and sent the letter to Polly in New York. I was not seriously thinking about going to Boston.

Ignorant bumpkin that I was, I didn't know that this dame in Boston was in charge of the book depart-ment at Jordan Marsh, New England's largest depart-ment store, and the "authors' luncheon" was her gim-mick to stimulate the sale of books. Accordingly, I didn't know that Polly Street had been working her head to the bone to get me on that program. Polly's telegram, telephoned to the farm next day by the Western Union office in Lewiston, said, "You go." So I went, and I was glad I did — because I didn't have to face anything like that again. I became an author in the golden ballroom of the Copley Plaza.

On the day of this authors' luncheon, I finished milking, had a good breakfast, and plowed the dooryard after an eighteen-inch February snowstorm. The morning was so cold I couldn't start our 1931 Model A on the battery, so my wife pushed it with the tractor until it coughed, and I took off for Brunswick, twelve miles away, to catch a train. The Ford would be waiting at the depot when I returned in the evening. The Jordan Marsh woman was waiting for me at the Copley Plaza. "Good of you to come," she said.

The ornate ballroom filled just before noon with an eager assembly of typical Boston ladies — of both sexes — who had paid, I learned, five dollars each for this cultural experience. The experience was a lunch and three authors who were to tell how they wrote their books. There could be no better place to become an author, and no better audience to assist. All the little Boston ladies wore hats. ("We don't buy our hats — we *have* our hats.")

They had the little lace choke collars.

Each was carrying *The Atlantic Monthly*.

They wore Ground Gripper shoes.

They had the S. S. Pierce breath.

So they luncheoned and looked forward to the stirring remarks of us authors, who were on exhibition at the head table and trying to look literary. The woman from Jordan Marsh said we would have fifteen minutes apiece, and we should explain how we wrote our books. One of us was a young fellow named Davis who taught in a college in New York State and had written a book about General Eisenhower. This was truly prophetic. At that time Ike was just another general mopping up Europe. The second author was Laurie Hillyer from New Hampshire, and I seem to recall her book's title was *Time Remembered.* I brought up the rear. The only things we three had in common were our books on sale at Jordan Marsh and the fact that until now none had heard of the others. Some professor from a college in Boston had been persuaded to introduce us, and I was familiar with the book from which he lifted his anecdotes. He told the stories well; I had never heard them told better.

Davis went first. He told how he had recognized Eisenhower as a comer, and how he researched him: He went to West Point for facts and got more from the War Department. He visited Kansas and Texas to get Eisenhower's family background. Then he went to Europe, and his efforts were crowned by an interview with Ike himself. There came a day, he told the Boston ladies, when he was quite ready and now all he had to do was write the book. He repaired to his "study." In creative surroundings he turned out the manuscript, which was edited and revised and rewritten. At last it was set in type and manufactured, and it was on sale at Jordan Marsh, and he had used up fourteen minutes and sixty seconds so he sat down.

He was rewarded by a furious flurry of polite Boston applause. Those ladies were some pleased.

They had paid five dollars for this, and by God they were going to enjoy it if it killed them. Boston applause is loud enough to be heard, but never rude and overdone. Little fingers are held aloof so they won't be involved in the clapping. Now the professor told a rousing good joke about Daniel Webster, because he was from New Hampshire and so was Laurie Hillyer, who needed no introduction but who was now introduced.

I liked her. I liked her fine. She was what my mother calls a "good, hearty woman," and New Hampshire is the next-best thing to Maine. But as she spoke, it became clear that her way of writing was a lot like that of Davis. She wanted a book that would illustrate a little three-part quotation from some poem or other. The first part of the book illustrated "youth," which was the first part of the quotation. She communicated a good deal with her small daughter while working on this part, to get the feeling of youth. The second part was about "maturity," and she communicated with her husband on that part. Then everybody in Peterborough turned out to communicate about "life entire," and there was nothing more to do now but retire to the "study" and write the book. This seemed reasonable to me. I thus learned about studies, which in Maine seem to amount to a kitchen table. When the book was finished, it got edited and revised and rewritten, it was now on sale at Jordan Marsh, and fifteen minutes had passed. The Boston ladies responded with another genteel ripple of appreciation.

8

It was my turn. I had meant to do about as the others. I had thought up some scholarly remarks that sounded good to me when I ran through them at milking time, and I thought the cow was attentive, too. But as I bowed at the professor, I changed my mind. I felt the time was right for the State o' Maine to take over. So I began: "This has been a moving experience for me. Up in Maine we don't have all the great advantages, and I never knew just how books were written until I listened today. We don't write books in Maine. We *live* books. We go hunting and fishing, we tend out on Grange meetings, we socialize as time permits, and after we've done enough living in Maine the pile is big enough and we send it to a publisher. That's it."

It was great fun to watch the ladies when this came out. Nobody before had ever said any such a thing at the literary luncheons in the Copley Plaza ballroom. Some of the ladies turned their heads cautiously in their lace choke collars, to see if a neighbor was betraying surprise.

"I'll give you an example," I said. I told them how my wife had pushed the Model A, and how I had come coughing down off Lisbon Ridge to turn onto State Highway 125, and how I had found Walter Keith standing there in the frigid dawn flailing his arms to keep warm and looking as if he wanted a ride.

"You don't know Walter Keith," I said. "He's a neighbor lives over on the Rabbit Road, he lives in a tar-paper woodchopper's shanty, and he does his own housekeeping and cooking. In Maine [I said] everybody is either an author or a character, and sometimes it's hard to tell us apart, but to a Maine author, Walter is what we call a Maine character. Walter is book material.

"So here I am, doing nothing more literary than going to catch a train, and all at once I have my next chapter sitting in my automobile all cocked and primed to help write my next book."

By this time the ladies were getting the hang of the thing, and they perked up some. I heard a smallish titter. And every word I spoke was the truth, because Walter gave me a chapter.

"As a Maine author," I said, "I have nothing whatever to do now but listen. You will notice the high quality of my approach. Since it is unusual to find Walter Keith standing in the road at eighteen below zero on a February morning, the literary requirements were aided by simple curiosity, so I had only to ask, 'Where're you goin', Walt?'

"To this straightforward approach, Walter replied in kind. He said, 'I'm goin' to town to buy myself some pastry.'

"Now, I've just told you that Walter did his own cooking, so the ingredients of a smallish plot are unfolding, or whatever it is ingredients do for authors. All I, the author, had to do was keep the ball on Walter's side of the net, so I lobbed back the most literary remark I could think of at the time. I said, 'Thought you did your own cookin'!'

"Walter said, 'Gen'ally I do, but my oven door's broke off.'

"This [I told the ladies] is basically what any high-school teacher of English composition would identify as the catastrophe, and it must be logically escorted to a satisfactory solution. I thereupon said to Walter that I would presume his well-known flair for Yankee ingenuity could easily overcome a minor problem like that."

Telling the rest, here on a printed page, is different from telling it to an audience of ladies in the ballroom of the Copley Plaza three decades ago. While I was getting the most out of Walter Keith, I was getting quite a good bit from the ladies. They were leaning forward now, and at one of the back tables a pair of opera glasses appeared. Right now literature stood still until Walter's Yankee ingenuity should reconcile his culinary catastrophe.

I quoted Walt. "Walter said, 'Well, I tried. I mixed some cake batter and some cookie dough, and where I couldn't bake it off — I fried it.'

"And now you can see how we authors in Maine pursue the muses. Author or not, the next question is one everybody will ask: 'How'd it taste?'

"Walter said, 'Just like fritters, b'god!' "

I drew the right conclusions from this, making my truly valid point that after one has given enough rides to enough Walter Keiths, the book is inevitable — a book that rather much wrote itself. No work; just fun. I added that we'd had a mild winter in Maine — it went down to forty-five below zero only twice, and then only for a week at a time. I said the snow clogged the fans on the Warren windmill, but a crew shoveled down and got the blades turning again. Bostonians love to hear about rugged Maine winters. I had used up maybe nine minutes, and I sat down. If applause measures success, I rated with Davis and Hillyer.

Then the professor said for a few minutes the folks might visit with our distinguished authors, and quite a few ladies came forward. One singled me out, and came charging up as if starting a Sears walk to Providence, thrusting a hand that sparkled with heirlooms. She was a thousand percent Beacon Hill. She pumped my hand as if priming a well, and she said something to me that nobody else has ever said. (There are words and expressions that get written, but never get spoken. The best example is "Alas!" Distraught females in all manner of novels have wrung their hands and cried, "Alas!" But nobody yet has actually said, "Alas!") What this Boston lady said was: "My good man!"

"My good man!" she said, "we do *so* love your Maine! We've passed forty-two seasons at Baw Hawbor!"

I said I thought that ought to be enough.

She didn't know what I meant.

But I did.

There are altogether too many places in Maine where the natural literary potentials, which amount to my bread and butter, have been sloughed off by too many people who have passed too many seasons. There are fine people in Bah Hah-b'h and I know many of them, but it's rare you'll pick up a Walter Keith at that crossroads.

I came home, and in spite of me Jordan Marsh did well with the book. The weather had softened somewhat, so the Model A kicked over and I got home in time for the barn work. My wife was in the kitchen, her feet in the oven of the range; she was reading a biography of Talleyrand, and she asked, "How'd things go?"

"They didn't believe a word I said."

"That's not important — did they have fun?"

"I don't rightly know."

"Well, did *you* have fun?"

"I always have fun."

"That's all that matters."

2

IT WAS NOT, as has been said, the Brain Trust of Franklin Delano Roosevelt's New Deal that put gobbledegook into Americanese and began the erosion of our language. Instead, this crime was perpetrated by the 1862 act of Congress that created the Department of Agriculture. This act established the land-grant colleges and the Extension Service; the intention was to bring information and culture to the farmers out on the land, who supposedly were intellectually starving and thirsting for knowledge. The government bulletin was invented. Available free for the asking, the government bulletins were written by "experts" who knew everything except how to write. There wasn't one in five hundred of the pen-pushing professors who had grounding in the gentle art of composition — however much they knew about manuring celery, breeding hogs, building henhouses, preserving kumquats, and fly-proofing privies.

The essence of gobbledegook appeared at once. A professor in a cow college would isolate the biodegradability factors in the bacterial composition of bovine lacteal fluids, and he would pass to the typewriter and whip off a bulletin. Without any kind of editing, the public printer would bring the thing forth at the taxpayers' expense, and the Extension Service would mail it postage-free to the thirsting farmers. Every farmer in the United States knew that milk will sour, and he now had it confirmed in elegant language. Early bulletins included *The Cumulative Effect of Fungicidal Treatment, Factors of Economy in Preparing Agrarian Cuisine,* and *Fertility Status of Soils Relating to Increment and Exhaustion of Nitrogen Sources.*

These bulletins became status symbols in the academic community — the first offenders in the "publish or perish" doctrine of faculty priorities. It is outrageous that so-called institutions of learning nurtured this bastard art, and that capped-and-gowned professors practiced it. Any student of American letters, and anybody "interested in writing," should study the government bulletin as the supreme bad example.

The first thing to be observed is the stupid fascination for big words. No bulletin yet has ever *used* anything; the word is *utilize*. Chicken feed is *nutriments*.

Feeding the pigs is *administering nutrimental concentrates and roughages*. A favorite bulletin word is *factor*, and while a factor should be an exact part of a conclusion, one professor found that a "factor" in mowing hay is the "custom of the driver." This means that Charlie drives the horses faster than Hank does; a discerning author careful with his words might think twice about erecting this difference into a scientific formula. Another "factor" in mowing hay with horses was "other stops." (Horses like to pause while they urinate.) The third factor was "size of mowing machine."

The early bulletins established an irrevocable form based on 1-2-3 or A-B-C. There must, sometime, be something that can be considered in twos or in fours, but all government bulletins have an early sentence that says something like "Three types are common." One bulletin said "three types or methods are common." I suspect that professor didn't know what a type was, much less a method. This suspicion of mine rests somewhat on his topic — he was writing about cesspools.

From the first it has been the custom to begin each bulletin with a short history of the subject. One bulletin about improving farm woodlots started off: "The American forest-products industry commenced when the good ship *Pied Cowe* loaded at Pipestave Landing." It occurs to me that a competent writer might take that line and bring forth a real Kenneth Roberts historical novel, but the professor thus covered the history of his topic and then trailed off into scaling tables and pine blister rust. (I've wondered if the *Pied Cowe* truly was a "good ship" — or was the professor beguiled by a tritie?)

Gathering factorial designs to support a bulletin is known as "confounding statistics." Not long ago two professors who couldn't think of anything else to gather factorial designs about gathered factorial designs about that, and their treatise on confounding statistics brought everything full circle: their government bulletin told how to prepare government bulletins. In taking soil samples, it advised, one must take many and find an average — a single sample might coincide with a spot where a squirrel peed, and you'd have the richest soil in the world, or "fertility status." In spite of this helpful, widely available treatise, a recent bulletin "averaged" the ratio of male to female in the deer harvest, and another "averaged" the number of times a glass milk bottle gets broken. Another speaks of "selected random numbers."

The student will be interested in the government bulletin's preoccupation with the footnote, the figure, the diagram, and the appendix. An experienced writer knows he shouldn't fool around with the attention of his reader. If you've got a reader, hang on to him. Don't, just when you've got him excited, stick in an asterisk and divert his attention. But with footnotes, figures, diagrams, and appendices, the professors keep their readers hopping all around. A bulletin on packaging "pomological products" (apples) ended a paragraph with this: ". . . amongst other factors. (See Fig. 12.)" Figure 12 (which was just a picture) had a footnote, and the footnote said to see the appendix. After all that, a reader might be led astray.

Telling a professor he can't write doesn't appeal to me. Suggesting any kind of editing would insult the learned man. Besides, the government bulletin has good intent, and even the worst of them have important information — although it can be obscured by "factors" and "types" and "statistical designs," and usually it is. The government bulletin turned farming to "agriculture," agriculture to "agronomy," and agronomy to "nonurban production service," and it wrought a big change in our language. People who object to *finalize* and all such ugly dalliance with our good mother tongue, should give credit where credit is due.

The student of composition perusing government bulletins to find out what not to do will discover they are not without a major redeeming "factor" — they are loaded with that best of amusements, unconscious humor. So seriously intent on his confounding of factorial designs, and so lacking in the rudiments of prose and poetry, the professor pays no attention to what he, himself, hath set down. The dissertation on cesspools (cesspools have now become "sanitary disposal systems") says that summer visitors to the homestead will not affect the efficiency of the disposal system.

Without the slightest doubt, the funniest unconscious humor any government bulletin has offered was
a study of toilet postures issued by the Extension Service of the University of Maine. It began innocently
enough as a set of instructions to people planning
bathrooms, and offered such bland information as the
fact that a toilet should stand out from the wall nineteen inches. Fine, so far. Soon, the reader was en-
grossed in some strange situations — people were
milling around this professor's clinical bathroom in
unprecedented numbers, brushing their teeth so it in-
terfered with somebody in the tub or somebody else
sitting on the hopper. The bulletin was illustrated
with the usual "figures," and in this instance the word
was apt. Young ladies, presumably students at the
university who had assisted in the confounding of
factorial designs, posed for photographs — modestly
blindfolded so readers would not recognize them. A
caption under one such photograph said:

> *Fig. 12, above.* One of the postures
> used to predict the elbow room needed
> while seated at the toilet.

The young lady was seated, elbows up, on a simulated
flush hopper.

In the ancient days of darkness and ignorance, the
country backhouse always had a "children's hole."
James Whitcomb Riley noted that in his celebrated
paean to the privy. There came a day when a child
was ready for the grown-ups' hole, and as it was some-

what larger than his baby perch, the safety admonition called to him when he went to the backhouse was "Keep your elbows up!" This has come over into Maine speech as a jocular warning in almost any situation — if you keep your elbows up, you won't fall through. Here was a young lady with her elbows up, and the professor was saying without the slightest touch of a smile, "Predicted: One-half of the hands-on-hips span if the front of the lavatory installation extends beyond a line through the greatest width of the opening in the toilet seat, but a lesser distance if the front of the lavatory is to the rear of this line."

The bulletin on toilet dimensions had a short life. It was so unconsciously hilarious that people who had no intention of building a bathroom sent for it, and more than a few disgusted taxpayers asked what was going on, anyway? After a time, folks who wrote to ask for a copy were told the edition had been exhausted.

I first became a student of the government bulletin when I was in high school and joined the 4-H Club. My father had always kept a flock of hens and I tended them much of the time. We had a henhouse, we fed the hens, we picked up eggs, and we picked Sunday dinners. Then I joined the 4-H Club and signed up for "poultry management," which called for a "poultryhouse," and we administered nutriments, tabulated ovulations, and salvaged protein edibles. I noticed this at the time I was scholastically involved with synechdochical accusatives and passive peri-phrastics, and I thought it was amusing. I'd start for the henhouse with a dish of swill, and arrive at the poultryhouse with a utensile of supplementary house-hold nutrients.

By the time I was writing my first little stories for the papers, I had a snide notion that someday I would do a bit of satire about professors who write bulletins, and I had quite a stack of horrible examples along the wall of my room. Then came the artificial insemina-tion of dairy cattle, and a wholly new "factor" came into play. The "unnatural" breeding of cows was re-sisted at first, and the dairy specialists had a bit of a task convincing farmers the method should be em-braced. There was a bit of a bawdy flavor to the whole thing, so the professors had to adapt their ornate bulletin verbosity so it doubled as euphemism. For the first time, they were not just talking around something for the sake of big words. One of the bulletins that urged acceptance of artificial insemination was so delicately wrought, and so badly written, that I pinned part of it to the wall over my typewriter as an admonishment.

It was a confounding of statistics to prove that a dairy farm cannot afford to maintain its herd bull once artificial insemination is available. All the factors were arrayed. It costs so much per square foot for stall space. Depreciation, repairs, and upkeep must be shared by the bull. He consumes hay, feed, and water; charge him for it. The professor also charged off against the bull his prorated share of the farm's monthly telephone bill. (That, in time, led to chapter two of my book *Farmer Takes a Wife*, where Oscar, the bull, telephones to Aunt Hulda in Cleveland.) The general nicey-nice confounding of the dairy bulletins during this crusade led to my satirical attack — and to one of the pleasantest lead balloons of my career.

The idea jelled when the International Harvester Company established its farm museum at Chicago. Visitors could see all manner of farm-related exhibits — with stuffed specimens of animals. The publicity about the new museum included a picture of a taxidermist attaching a horn to an otherwise finished dairy cow.

Aha!

I started at once on my government bulletin to expose government bulletins. I confounded my factorial designs, selected my footnotes and figures, decided on my three types (or methods), and researched my history of the subject. With the photograph of the taxidermist setting the horn, I developed proof that bovine lacteal fluid production could be increased by changing the angles of a cow's horns. Then I promoted myself to a full professorship and invented a college. I felt I'd finished a good piece — and now, where to send it?

Mostly, when a writer starts a piece, he has some idea about its market. It's wise to aim at something. But I just couldn't see the staid farm publications jumping up and down about this one. *Country Gentle-*

man was then in business but said no. No, also, from *Farm Journal.* I didn't bother with *New England Homestead* and *Rural New Yorker.* They wouldn't know what to do with it. But writers should not despair. In 1946 there appeared a new kind of farm magazine — a slick, put out in Cincinnati by a long-establish publisher of other magazines. Called *The Farm Quarterly,* its first issue suggested to me that its editors might like a spoof on professors and government bulletins.

The late Fred Knoop was managing editor of *The Farm Quarterly,* and he was so pleased with my "government bulletin" that he sent me the biggest check I had yet received for writing and hustled my study of horn elevation into the winter issue of 1946.

All hell broke loose.

A Study of Cumulative Results in Dairy Improvement on Maine Farms by Horn Elevation.

By Professor John Gould
University of Lisbon, Maine

THE history of horn elevating may be divided, roughly, into three periods. The earliest reference in historical writings comes in Holy Scripture where God commanded the lifting up of horns, as a result of which Hemen (whose name is apt) sired 14 sons and 3 daughters. This period offers small information to the dairy farmer and technician, and is interesting only cursorially.

The second period extends from

about 75 B.C. to the landing of the
Pilgrims, which was in 1620 at Ply-
mouth, Massachusetts. The third period brings us up to date, and includes
the election of James K. Polk. It was
not until 1939 that elevating horns of
dairy cattle was considered a factor
in dairy improvement. Research at
Lisbon University establishes the affin-
ity between milk production and horn
elevation.

Accidental Polling

Opportunity to investigate horn
elevating came when a scrub Ayer-
shire in the barn of Telesphore
Plourde, Peppermint Corner, Maine,
knocked off her horns trying to get
out of the barn. Mr. Plourde called on
members of the University staff who
cornered the cow in upper Oxford
County and replaced the lost horns.
Mr. Plourde observed and mentioned
that the angle of adjustment was
about 13½ degrees in excess of the
original angle, but aside from giving
the heifer a slightly startled appearance the general aspect was not inferior to the former stance.

Lactation Commences

This cow, whose name was Lulu,
came in heat the following Monday,

and was bred artificially to Rufus High Barclay's Petunia's Lad II. She threw triplet bull calves, and freshened with 21.6 to 21.7 pounds per milking, at 6-hour intervals. At the time the University staff did not find this noteworthy, but they became interested when Mr. Plourde stated that the heifer's mother had never given more than a quart of milk a day, was always bred with difficulty, and his wife had frequently complained that it took 37 gallons of her milk to make one small pat of inferior butter.

Was Elevation a Factor?

This astonishing improvement in a single generation was immediately of interest, and students at the University made frequent research excursions to the Plourde dairy. Careful studies revealed that the new elevation of Lulu's horns was the only accountable factor in the increased milk production.

Diet Studies

Lulu was given successively reductive nutriments, varying from complete roughages, with intermediate admixtures of computed values, but her production figure remained constant. (See Table I)

Table I

Feed	Amount	Results
Mixture A	2 quarts	Good
B	"	"
C	"	"
D	"	"
E	"	"
F	"	"

Other factors, such as pasturage, water, milking time, and temperature were likewise found to be nil. When horn elevation was deduced to be the causative factor, experiments were conducted to determine which angle of horn attachment would produce the greatest desired effect.

Various Angles

Table II shows the remarkable increase in milk production over a 7-month period as the horns of Lulu were successively raised from their second position to that ultimately considered the maximum.

Table II

Angle of Lift	Pounds Produced
32 degrees	76
78 "	128
82 "	156
101 "	167
127 "	202
156 "	313
180 "	582

At the completion of the seventh elevation Lulu's horns were sticking straight up in the air, were a bright green in color, and Lulu was dead. It could be assumed that overproduction had sapped every vestige of vitality, and the conclusion was drawn that elevating the horns above 82 degrees was likely to produce an abnormal strain on the alveoli.

Subject Renewed

In 1944 the study was revived. In that year a total of 130 cows in this area were given horn elevations, with a casualty rate of only 17%. Results tend to show that a corrected elevation of between 10 and 35 degrees, measured from a perpendicular to a line from the base of the left horn to the tip of the right horn, will double milk production within a period of three weeks. The right horn was chosen as the basis of operation, because rarely do both horns have an identical declination, and it was essential to unify the initiatory fundamentals.

Casualty Rate Reduced

No cow was found to have the correct angle from birth, although two cows were all right in one horn. It was believed only coincidence that in these two cases the right horn was the one at a proper angle. The casualty rate of 17% was eliminated almost at the second interval of adjustment, as operators found the horn is more safely removed by giving it a sharp rap with a baseball bat than by using a Stillson wrench to unscrew it.

Conclusions

Although observation tends to support the theory that all cows will produce more milk if their horns are set at the correct angle for the particular breed and the quantity of milk desired, experiments have not progressed far enough to establish that as an unalterable rule. Since milk production has been the object of this study, no horn elevations were attempted on bulls.

That's the way the thing read. The editors of *The Farm Quarterly* were no more ready for what happened than I was. We were all swamped with letters from the American farm community asking for further information on this amazing study. The simple truth was that our farm people had been so brainwashed by farm-bulletin lingo that they were quite ready to accept as gospel anything worded in that style — particularly if it originated in a university and was signed by a professor. I had over five hundred such letters. The editors wrote to ask me if I wanted them to forward the letters they got, but I said no — so I never knew how many came altogether.

At first I supposed some of those letter-writers were pulling my leg in return for my attempt to pull theirs — but too many of them enclosed self-addressed stamped envelopes for reply: when you do that, you're serious. A number of the letters were from professors — themselves heads of dairy departments at land-grant institutions. One letter (I have all these letters still, and can show them) came from the chief veterinarian of Swift & Company. I went around for some years afterwards using this horn-elevation article and the mail it prompted as fodder in after-dinner talks — it went over best before farm groups and seminars of "people interested in writing."

So one year the man who managed our Maine Breeding Cooperative was chairman for the annual convention of the artificial dairy inseminators of Canada, Mexico, and the United States. He set up a big meeting at the Marshall House at York Beach and asked me to come and speak. I did. I gave the horn-elevation story, and that was a perfect audience for it. The Marshall House rocked with laughter, and each burst teased me to try for a topper. I guess it was my best performance. Then I started to read some of the letters that asked for "further information" and "printed literature" and I came to the one from a professor who was head of the department of dairying at a western state university. The instant I read off his name, all hilarity ceased and the Marshall House went as quiet as the tomb — as still as the breast when the spirit has departed.

It was completely unnerving. I had nothing else to do but bring my remarks to a close, and I did. Then I learned that this professor had addressed the convention that very afternoon on the subject of nutritional factors in pregnancy diets, and that he was sitting right by me at the head table when I read off his name.

All of which was momentarily disconcerting — but afterwards it was part of the great fun it was, first to last, to spoof the government bulletin and satirize its gobbledegook. And I really did get a letter from that veterinarian — he wrote: "We will be anxiously awaiting receipt of this information and remain, very truly yours, SWIFT & COMPANY."

3

EVERY SCHOOLMARM who has tried to interest her little bahstids in composition and rhetoric gets the same question over and over again: "But what shall I write about?" It is not, really, a bad question. Experience teaches an alert writer not to send a manuscript about smallpox in ancient China to *Cricket*, but in the early throes of schoolroom creativity a youngster may well need a few helpful suggestions from Teacher. John Coggswell, who was a Sunday writer on the Boston *Post* and later under contract to the old *Saturday Evening Post*, was often asked how he decided what to write about, and he had a fine answer: "I work maybe three or four hours a day, but humanity is busy twenty-four hours a day, the clock around, year in and year out, thinking up things for me to write about. I'll never catch up."

One of my early efforts became folklore before its time, and I've used it as an example many times when young folks have asked how themes come about. Percy Pratt put the idea in my head.

In my growing-up in Freeport, Maine, the Pratts stood tall in the community. Everett, Percy's brother, stood about seven feet, and my father jested him one time about his height. Dad had a sugar maple on the front lawn and every spring he would put in two tap holes. Mother simmered the sap on the kitchen range, and the one tree always gave us enough maple syrup for the year. One spring it came time to tap and we had about eight feet of accumulated snow. Dad climbed up on the snowbank and bored his holes, put in his spiles, and hung his buckets.

Within a week the snow was gone and we had bare ground. So Dad would go out with a stepladder to collect his sap, and as he was up there one day Everett Pratt came strolling by.

"Gracious, Frank," said Everett, "why in the world did you hang your buckets so high off the ground?"

Dad said, "Well, if anybody pees in my pails, I'll know who did it."

Everett was not amused, and said so; it was not the kind of ribaldry one used with the Pratts. They were fine people. "The Pratt girls" were tall, but not so tall as the boys. Percy and his brother Osborne were not so tall as Everett. Percy was a clerk in the post office, and during World War II became famous the world around as a poet.

When the Freeport boys began going off to war, Percy got their service addresses as a matter of routine, and he began mailing them a weekly letter from home — he mimeographed the thing and paid all the postage himself. Wherever a Freeport boy was, anywhere in the world, Percy kept him informed of goings-on back home. He put the news in the most inhumane doggerel since the Sweet Singer of Michigan, so utterly abusive to the art of prosody and versification that it was wonderful. It informed the Freeport boys of local affairs, but before long the mis-rhyme and broken meter became preferred reading matter to the entire military, whether they knew anything about Freeport or not. When Percy's doggerel came to a soldier, the whole regiment gathered. When Percy started, he had no idea the stunt would grow into a major chore, which it did. But he never failed the boys. The boys, in turn, wrote back to thank Percy, and told him how the weekly letters were so well received by the ranks. One day L. L. Bean said to Percy, "Perc, you're better known around the world than I be!" Such acclaim could not be ignored; after that the Freeport Lodge of Knights of Pythias sponsored Percy's "newspaper," paying for the mimeographing and the postage.

Here comes edition TWENTY,
The weather is forty below;

Having cold weather a-plenty,
Coldest Freeport did ever know.

The village square was filled with snow,
No men to shovel could be had,
But high school boys to work did go,
And they sure worked like mad.

Births, deaths, home-front hardships imposed by the OPA, changes in business ownerships, fires — Percy got them all in. It was long before he became world famous as the poet laureate of the GIs that I discovered Percy Pratt was a gold mine — my weekly gossip column in the Brunswick *Record* seldom went to press without something Percy had given me to "write about." One day I was talking through the post-office wicket to Percy, and Elwood Stowell, another clerk, came up and said, "Perc, tell John about your rat."

Percy had been bothered with rats in his henhouse, but hadn't done too well with cats and traps. Then he saw a rat's tail hanging down over a beam; the rat was hiding but forgot to tuck in his tail. Percy sneaked in his .22 rifle, lined it up on the beam so it would hit the rat, and pulled the trigger. Twelve rats dropped off the beam — they'd been lined up so Percy got them with one shot.

But a story like that is subject to revision and embellishment, and after I used it as a news item in the *Record* I kept it in mind for something else. I toyed around with the general idea of mass success when a gun goes off. When I had Percy's rats worked into a Sunday feature, I mailed it to the *Post* in Boston, and said to Percy, "You'll want to see this when it comes out — it's the latest version of your rat story."

The Sunday *Post* printed it in 1929. It was cribbed by nobody-knows-how-many other newspapers across the land, and was sometimes rewritten as a local happening. As it made the rounds, it happened in the Berkshires, in the Ozarks, in the Sierras, and frequently in the Prairie States. My name was no longer on it or associated with it. The story entered folklore and appeared in a scholarly anthology that reported it happened in Minnesota.

When at last I reworked it again and used it in *The Parables of Peter Partout,* the critic who reviewed that book for *The New York Times* accused me of stealing an old doozie out of the National Tradition. I believe any author has the right to steal his own material, and perhaps this background will explain to budding writers how anybody finds things to write about. Here's how Percy's rats wound up, a tale as tall as any Pratt:

Faithful to the End

Dear Mr. Editor:

A faithful dog is a great boon, but there are times when they overdo the amenities, and I am about to report a notable incident which I believe is unique in the annals of our society. You know my dog Roland. He is the one I swapped for an Oliver typewriter, if that means anything to today's uninformed millions, and it has always been a great question in my mind if I got stuck or not. Anyway, Roland has proved a faithful, if uninspired servant, and has grown old in the company of his master. He is always at my heels, whence arises the situation about to be described.

I've been having a little trouble with something in the henhouse. I don't know just what it is, but have decided it is either a fox or a weasel. During the night I would hear the hens making a commotion, but by the time I arrived to investigate, the marauder would have made off, and I have not really caught sight of him to know what it is. I did put some bait on a trap, and covered the trap with a box so the hens couldn't get at it, figuring if it's a weasel or a rat there might be some chance, but the thing was still shrouded in the mystery of a farmyard night, and I wotted not.

Well, the night before last I was enveloped in the connubial sheets, and four blankets, knitting up the raveled sleeve of care, as they say. Mrs. Partout was sleeping soundly, as is her wont, and I

37

was presumably doing the same. Good old Roland, nose cradled as usual in his paws, was curled up on the rug at the foot of the bed right where the moonlight came in at the window, ready at a moment's notice to rise and defend the castle, if he chanced to wake up.

At this moment I was aroused from the soporific state by the cackling of some hens, and I quietly laid the bedclothes back from my side and stepped out onto the floor. Every move I made was slow and methodical, as I intended to sneak silently out to the henhouse with my shotgun and take the law into my own hands, be it skunk, fox, owl, or thief. I realize now that I should have pulled on my pants, but I did not. I was sleeping in my long-legged underwear, which may not be the Emily Post fashion amongst the high born and the well bred, but which is a very good way to handle matters out here in the country where life is more forthright and the business of going to bed and getting up in a cold bedroom is a constant concern. I was wearing the kind which has a drop seat, which is a delicate thing to mention in this company, but I do want everybody to get the exact picture of just how this thing took place. The drop seat, I will add, was in the dropped, or open, position.

Now, I grant you that few people rise from a snug bed in their underwear and wander about, but I had been asleep, I had those hens on my mind, it was dark except for the moon, and the possibility of great numbers of people out behind my buildings to see me was remote. So I shoved my feet in my boots, paying no heed to anything else, and I took the shotgun from the corner, put in a load, and went out through the shed for the business I was then about. All, of course, in silence and stealth, slow step by slow step, and I opened the back door inch by inch.

What I did not know, in my concentration on purpose, was that my faithful dog Roland, waking as I left the bed, still half asleep and in his dotage, arose from the rug and followed at my heels. Taking each step as painstakingly as I did, he so accompanied me that I did not know he was there, and on I went with the utmost intent toward the henhouse. I stepped warily in the snow, so as not to crunch, and arrived at the door of the henhouse.

Careful not to fumble the hasp, I drew the peg, laid it quietly on the snow, opened the door a slight crack, thrust in the muzzle of the shotgun, and bent forward to peek inside to see what might be going on. All I could see was the white hens sitting in rows on the roosts, some of them still making an outcry over whatever it was that had disturbed them, and the moonlight on the floor as it came in the windows. Somewhere in the shadows, I was sure, there lurked the skunk or fox or whatever it was, and I squinted my eyes to see.

Now at this precise instant, faithful in his devotions, old Roland, who evidently had not perceived that my forward motion ceased at the door, came behind me and ran his cold nose through the trap in my underwear.

I am not going to try to describe the peculiar sensation this arouses in a sensitive person. I can only report that I at once discharged the shotgun, which mowed thirty-nine hens and two roosters off the perch, and that I spent the rest of that night and all the next day picking chickens. Mrs. Partout, with many a salty word, arose at the blast and having found out what happened began getting jars ready to can poultry meat. We have since completed this unexpected task, and I have hastened to take pen in hand and inform you at the first possible mo-

ment. I just wanted to say that sometimes a faithful old dog can be altogether
too faithful, and that I believe Roland
fits into that category.

(signed) *Peter Partout*
Peppermint Corner

4

THE WORLD is full of people like Percy Pratt who nourish the inspiration of attentive writers. Now and then they get an acknowledgment (as my uncle Ralph did from Kenneth Roberts for his help with the gangway pendulum in *Captain Caution*), but they share in no royalties and they get no academic degrees. I'm grateful to all the feeders I've known; they've kept me supplied with good yarns at no expense. One of my best, and probably the most improbable, was Clarence Dixon. Clarence died some time ago, and until his obituary appeared (which I wrote) few Freeporters knew his name was Clarence.

He was out of Nova Scotia, with seafaring background, and he was a hunchback. He stood barely four feet tall, so he had to stand on tiptoe to look over the coaming of his boat. Since he had a wharf and marine railway at South Freeport harbor, he was the logical man to be harbor master, an appointive town officer who amounted to a policeman for the waterfront. This office carried the honorary title of Captain, but Clarence also had his tickets for wind and steam in all waters. So he was known to his face as Cappy Dixon, and behind his back as Humpy Dixon, and his mother's choice of Clarence was forgotten. By the time I was writing and looking for inspiration, Cappy was running rum, as smuggling liquor was known as in the Volstead days. This was no secret to me, inasmuch as an alert young reporter keeps himself informed, but because Cappy had never been caught at it, it was privileged information — outside the public domain.

From the distance of a half-century, running rum may need an explanation. The Prohibition Amendment brought great activity and much prosperity to the coast of Maine. The innumerable bays, coves, guzzleholes, eel ruts, gunkholes, and coddes of the shoreline could not be patrolled by the enforcement officers. Maine seiners and lobstermen knew every reef and passage at every point of the tide; government agents who pursued them always sailed by the charts. Twenty-five hundred miles of Maine tidewater embraced prohibition wholeheartedly, and thirsts in Boston, Providence, New York, and as far as Baltimore, were assuaged. Larger vessels called mother ships would come down from Saint Pierre and New-foundland, loaded with everything from Screech to champagne, and would lay to about four miles off the Maine coast. So long as they stayed outside the three-mile limit, they were as safe as in church, and there they stayed waiting for small boats to come out and relieve them of cargo — usually in five-gallon square cans.

There was communication. Somebody knew where the mother ship would be, and somebody knew who would come out. The revenue officers couldn't seize liquor until it was inside the limit, so they'd wait until a loaded fishing boat pulled away from the mother ship and headed for shore. Then came a merry chase, more often than not with gunfire, but in the history of rum-running few of the chases were successful for the enforcers. The lobsterman would hit the tide just right, lightly touch his keel on a reef, and by the time the pursuers got to that reef it was a foot out of water. And by the time the pursuers consulted their charts and found another route into the gunkhole, the booze had been delivered and the lobsterman was home in bed.

Cappy Dixon ran a lot of rum. In the first place, his seamanship was superb — but he also had a special boat. She was the *Dolphin*, larger and heavier built than the fishing boats of the time, and she had power-ful twin diesels. The Coast Guard had nothing that could outrun the *Dolphin*. Cappy told me he could churn off thirty knots with a full load of five-gallon cans. But few knew just what Cappy had below decks of the *Dolphin*. Around the harbor, he chugged as if he had a one-lung Hartford, and many felt sorry for the poor cripple who perhaps didn't have money enough for an engine job. But the diesels were kept shining below and I happen to know (a reporter's privilege) that they could drag down the *Dolphin*'s stern in a most purposeful manner. Many times Cappy didn't bother with the mother ships, but ran up to Saint Pierre and Saint John's, stopping off in Nova Scotia to see his own aged mother.

I think it was in 1928 that Cappy Dixon decided to accompany Commander Donald B. MacMillan on one of his "Arctic expeditions." MacMillan, who had been on Peary's dash to the pole, had grown up in Freeport, and was the local hero. His schooner *Bowdoin*, built specially for his explorations, was new, and fittingly he decided to embark from Freeport. The town was to turn out and bid adieu, with the governor on hand, and it was a rousing send-off. I mean not to belittle Commander MacMillan, who was always "Cap'n Dan" to us fawning boys in Freeport, but it is true that by that time his trips to the North had become something of a summer adventure cruise for college boys who paid a fee. I wanted to go on one of his trips, but dissuaded myself when I learned the price. This in no way minimizes the importance of Cap'n Dan as an Arctic explorer — he took that seriously, and his student crews collected specimens, took soundings, and performed scientifically under his direction. Cap'n

Dan unquestionably brought home more valid and useful information about the Arctic than any five other explorers you can name. So he edged out of South Freeport harbor on his motor, and raised sail just off Crab Island, bound for Etah.

All the small craft in the harbor, stinkpot and sail, escorted the *Bowdoin* outside, flags flying, horns blatting, and cannon saluting, and amongst 'em was the *Dolphin*, chugging along in desultory fashion with Cappy Dixon's head just topping the coaming. One by one the other boats fell off and returned, but Cappy stayed astern.

MacMillan was a top-notch sailor, and he knew Cappy. He felt the outside breeze nudge his sails, and as the *Bowdoin* lowered her looard rail he supposed Cappy, being outdistanced, would turn back. But Cappy nudged his throttle and stayed on. When the *Bowdoin* put into Christmas Cove to pass her first night out, Cappy politely asked the harbor master for assignment of mooring, sir, and tied on. Up the Maine coast, night by night — Castine, Stonington, Cutler — Cappy stayed. Which he had every right to do, but MacMillan wasn't happy about the company. What kind of an expedition was this, when a lobster boat tagged along? It was in Harbour Grace that Cap'n Dan finally spoke the *Dolphin* with words of advice, and plainly told Cappy he was no longer truly welcome.

Cappy was not offended. He took on some square five-gallon cans of new-run Newfie Screech and came home. He told me: "Gracious me! I had no idea I was intrudin'. I pulled killick and put. Last thing I'd do is offend Cap'n Dan!"

Cappy was articulate, with good diction and a full vocabulary. He would use many words I had to look up afterwards. Considering his size, his baritone voice seemed overloud, and he would have made a great orator in the days before microphones. His meager Bluenose education must have been a good one. He had an absolute gift of narrative, and a great sense of suspense — lighting his pipe was pure drama. He was as good as O. Henry at holding a snapper to the end. I came to realize he welcomed my company — even though he well knew I was picking his mind — because not too many people cottoned to his misshapen back, and because too many others disapproved of his illicit traffic. I would pick up a pound of tobacco — it cost seventy-five cents, then — and lope into his little "poop deck" on his wharf. His housekeeping was nasty neat. I'd set the can of tobacco on his table, he'd nod at the other rocker, and we'd have at it. It got so I had only to say, "I need a yarn."

Cappy came to give forethought to my visits and would be ready. One afternoon his door was open and he was sitting with cat on knee, looking over the harbor. Most of the fishing boats had come in and were on mooring. The channel between Punkin Nub and Pound o' Tea led like a path for the eyes into the ocean, with a slender, almost invisible line that was the tower on Halfway Rock. Beyond that was Spain.

And just this side of Crab Island Marty Holbrook had a peapod with a hogshead amidships — he was jigging for bait pollock, and we could see him slat them into the barrel. Cappy said, "Whyn't you do a story on how a simple harbor master outranks an admiral in the Younited States Navy?"

"Go ahead," I said.

"Well, I was sittin' just like this, Tabby on my knee, and it was just such a beautiful afternoon. You don't see Halfway Rock from here too often. I must have dozed, and somethin' bothered Tabby so she stuck in her pins. I looked up, and here was a warship comin' in."

South Freeport harbor has good draft, so that was all right, but there hadn't been a warship in the harbor since the *Dash* was built there for the War of 1812 — and she wasn't really a warship, she was a privateer. Well, Cappy said, in no time at all curiosity had everybody lined up along the shore, and quite a few went out in small boats for a closer look. The warship dropped anchor over on the Staples Point side, and a sailor with a megaphone began warning the small boats to stay clear. Cappy watched all this, and after a time he set Tabby down, pulled on his boots, went down the ladder on his wharf, and rowed his skiff out to the warship.

He had surmised she was a destroyer, but as he came nearer she looked more like a light cruiser. The sailor came to the rail and warned Cappy away, but Cappy kept right on rowing. Push-rowing, of course — so he was facing the warship and he saw the sailor had a gun. "Final warning!" shouted the sailor.

Cappy certainly had no appearance of authority. I've pondered on that sailor's thoughts as he saw Cappy's meager bulk and humped jacket. Cappy kept coming and the sailor did not shoot. "Hold your fire, matey," yelled Cappy. "I'm harbor master!"

The sailor called, "Stay where you are!" and disappeared. In just about a minute he was back at the rail, and with him an officer in full ceremonial uniform. Cappy said, "A reg'lar spit-'n'-polish cockatoo in a fore-'n'-aft hat." Cappy said this spectacle did sort of take him by surprise, and not knowing what else to do he shipped his laboring oar and saluted. Then he called, "Cap'n Clarence Dixon at your service, sir — request permission to come aboard! Official inspection! Harbor master, sir!"

Cappy said everybody fell to. Officers lined up, seamen secured the ladder, and as Cappy reached the tumble home somebody piped him aboard. The officer in the John Paul Jones hat shook Cappy's hand, welcomed him, and asked, "*What* is a harbor master?"

Cappy said, "I politely thanked them one and all, welcomed them on behalf of the municipal officers, and said, 'A harbor master is the duly appointed and qualified town officer responsible for a tight harbor — it's my duty to check your anchorage, sir.'"

At that, Cappy said, everybody started to laugh, and they all shook his hand, and they bade him aft and bought him a drink. Turned out this cruiser had been on one of these trial runs, after a big commissioning party, and she'd blown an engine gasket or something. They came into Freeport on half-power for repairs. They explained to Cappy that ordinarily this class of vessel didn't carry a full admiral, but because of the commissioning ceremony, one had chanced to be aboard. Cappy stayed until late in the evening, giving the admiral some valuable tips on navigating. Had mess with the admiral, too. And quite a few snorts. When it came time to leave, the admiral himself handled the oars in Cappy's skiff, and Cappy and all the officers and the admiral himself stood up, in the down-east fashion. People on shore heard them singing as they came — a ditty Cappy had taught them:

> *We're the girls from Antigonish,*
> *We know how to clean the fish . . .*

The cruiser's gig came to return the officers to the ship, and Cappy called a nautical good-night as they sped away.

"Got a Christmas card from that admiral, year after year," Cappy told me. "Never forgot the good time we gave him in Freeport. Shows that at times a harbor master can outrank an admiral in the Younited States Navy!"

Unable to catch Cappy at rum-running, the officers in desperation finally resorted to a "plant." This consisted of putting a pint of whiskey in Cappy's jacket pocket as it hung on a hook in the town-hall cloakroom. Cappy was attending town meeting. When he came out and put on his jacket they arrested him for "illegal possession." Cappy spent a year in Danbury Penitentiary. He made no defense; he didn't even try to explain. No need — he knew it was a plant, the officers knew it was a plant, everybody in town knew it was a plant. But the same people — Cappy, the cops, and the citizens — also knew about the thousands and thousands of times Cappy hadn't been caught. After he came home he told me: "They didn't catch me fair. They should have caught me fair."

The last time I saw Cappy he had suffered a small stroke and lost his speech. He was in a rocking chair, cat on his knee. I put the can of tobacco on the table at his elbow and he nodded. There would be no more stories.

5

I T'S A WISTFUL kind of pleasure to sit as I do and reflect on the people and things that helped me be a writer. Good friends and good folks, their place in literature is somewhat that of a caddy at golf — and I've heard it said the caddy makes the champion. Flint Johnson, I think, is the only caddy I maligned to the extent that I needed a fake name for him. He has appeared as "Flats Jackson" time and time again. Usually, he could have sued my pants off if I'd called him Flint Johnson, a risk I didn't care to run even though I knew absolutely Flint wasn't the suing kind. The reason for this caution is that Flint suggested situations rather than gave me yarns as Cappy Dixon did. Before I worked them into salable manuscripts

I had generally developed the person Flint into the character Flats, and Flats would be one jump ahead of the game warden. Taking a Flint Johnson story to the typewriter and coming away with a Flats Jackson piece gives the lie to the theory that writing is hard work. It has always been a pleasure to dabble with Flats — or Flint.

I met Flint on the seventeenth of May, 1949. Curt Mercer and I had been up Kennebago Stream hunting trout. Curt, who had a set of camps and a tenting area on big Rangeley Lake, had a drinking problem. The rum he took stirred up his stomach ulcer, creating the problem. He had doctored for this problem, and the doctor told him to drink milk. After that, Curt put the rum in milk, but he couldn't see that it made that much difference. Some people thought that when Curt's time came, it was the milk that did it. Curt and I were congenial, and went fishing together many times.

On that fateful seventeenth of May, we cadged a Rangeley boat at the Oquossoc Angling Club, and went up past Indian Rock to try some rips. We got to Screw Auger Falls to go ashore and have our lunch, and while eating I flicked a fly out. There was an explosion that is unique in my angling career, and I stayed right there on that trout for forty-five minutes. Curt netted him, and we decided we had a trophy fish and I should take him to Herbie Welch for mounting. That fish is on my "study" wall as I write — he weighed six-and-one-half pounds, hit twenty-four inches in length, the largest trout of my life. He was also, for what it means, the last trout Herbie Welch mounted entirely by himself. Herbie, onetime baseball player, sometime taxidermist, and full-time fly-casting champion of the world, was aging and had taken in an apprentice to help him stuff. After my trout, Herbie never did another completely by himself.

When Curt and I got back to Indian Rock with this trout, it created a sensation. Time was that trout from six to nine pounds were everyday in the Rangeley region, but that time was long gone. If we'd come back without the fish, and claimed we'd seen a twenty-four-inch baister, nobody would have believed us. But here he was in the boat. One dear lady, member of the Oquossoc Angling Club, wrung my hand and said: "I've been coming here since 'ninety-eight, every single year, hoping for such a fish and I never got one. I'm proud to shake the hand of a man who did!" When I turned back from the lady, my trout was gone. I looked about — we'd collected maybe a dozen people on the wharf — and my trout wasn't in the crowd. I said to Curt, "Somebody snatched Fontinalis!"

"Flint Johnson," he said.

Curt showed no concern. It was pretty near an hour when Flint Johnson brought my trout back — he'd taken it over to Oquossoc, over to Haines Landing, and even into Rangeley Village to show it to everybody he could find. Now Curt said, "Here's Flint."

Flint is a huge man, with the oddity of no bridge to his nose. His nose comes right off his forehead and his eyebrows run straight across. His powerful shoulders are hung with heavy and strong arms, and he grabbed my hand in one of his so his fingers wrapped right around and overlapped. He waltzed me all around the dock in exuberant delight. Like the little lady, he was proud to shake the hand of a man who did. If Flint had caught that trout himself, he could have been no more happy. Something he said caused Curt and me and the trout to include Flint in our success, and after we took the fish to Herbie Welch we went to Flint's home in Boobytown, just outside Rangeley Village. There I met Flint's amiable and comely wife, Red, who was just as happy for me as Flint had been, and she prepared a bountiful supper, which we drank ravenously. Curt and I insisted on bringing the exercises to a conclusion at two-thirty the next morning, but the program was enough to make me and the Johnsons friends for life, and me the debtor for untold inspiration.

I believe Flint to be the best woodsman in Maine. He has super-extra senses. I've been with him on the trail when he would shush me, point, and after four or five seconds a deer would walk from a thicket. How he knew that deer would be there or would come forth is a good question. Once, on a long hike, I said a drink of water would go good. Flint sniffed, walked off the trail, scratched in the ground, and found a spring. He scooped dirt away, and after the mud settled we had a drink so cold it ached my teeth. He knew how to find water. On a stream, he'd take a trout with every cast — none wasted. "If you understand how trout feed," he said, "you'll know where they are — no sense whipping a fly on an empty pool."

Flint originated in what he calls "the wooden country," but at one time drove a taxi in Brooklyn. His wife is a registered nurse. They once owned a set of sporting camps on Spencer Stream, and have operated others. He has been a chopper, a teamster, a river driver, a cook. He has cruised timber lots, cut Christmas trees, worked on timberland roads. Lately he has "worked on the mountain," which consists of handling the machinery at the Saddleback ski area. He has no peer in handling a canoe, poling or on paddle, and I've made the entire Allagash River trip with him. The woods of Maine have been my favorite topic, and a great deal of my understanding of them came through Flint.

But, you see, there is something about the Maine woods that calls for embellishment, and this is why I invented the somewhat unethical Flats Jackson, who can poach a deer for the outdoors magazines without getting Flint Johnson in trouble.

Flint and I had been up on Kibby Stream one day to see if the trout were holding up, and on the way home we came through the town of New Vineyard. Just outside town, Flint roused from a doze, looked to see where we were, and said, "Just up ahead here, you look to the right and you'll see a big pine tree all by itself on a knoll."

Sure enough, there was the pine. "One time I was

coming along here, and I saw five deer standing in a cluster under that tree."

He dwelt in his mind's eye for a moment and I drove along. Then he said, "Handsomest sight I ever saw. Late September, so the law was on and they weren't shy. Two bucks, two does, and a spikehorn. Beautiful!"

I drove along.

Flint said, "You know — it's one helluva job to dress out five deer all at once!"

So you can see why I invented Flats Jackson.

Flint gave me the idea for the smelt story. Flats had a twitchin' horse (for dragging logs out of the woods), and he stepped to the stable after dark to give the horse a drink. He picked up a pail and went to the brook. Just as he was about to dip, somebody in the dark, unrecognizable, jostled him, dumped a netful of smelts into the pail, and took off like a whippet into the night. Whoever it was, he had detected the approach of a game warden on the other side of the brook and in this way had disposed of the evidence. Flats was caught red-handed with a pailful of illegal smelts. I have always been fond of the closing line: "Flats said, 'I'm the only man in the State o' Maine ever got fined for waterin' his twitchin' horse!'"

Sometimes I haven't bothered to separate the Flints from the Flats. One time Flint was driving toward Wilton and saw a huge buck cross the road ahead of him. He braked, got a shell into his rifle, and stood on the shoulder of the road, looking into the woods. He saw hair, and fired. Turned out to be a yearling, not the buck he had seen. And as he was dressing this midget out, the owner of the land appeared with a game warden and Flint was arrested for hunting on posted land. Flint had no way of knowing, as there was no KEEP OFF sign right where this all happened, but the owner was one of these city castoffs with more money than brains, and he had a deep sense of possession and a great hatred for anybody who likes venison. Flint, or maybe it was Flats, said, "Damned little lamb, weighed twenty-eight pounds dressed out, and we ate the whole thing for Thanksgiving dinner. Including costs, the meal came to three hundred and sixty-eight dollars."

If these incidents indicate Flint was a hard-luck artist in his relations with the fish-and-game commissioner, I wouldn't be surprised. There was one fall the wardens were definitely out to get him. He'd had his guide's license lifted on account of the smelt caper, and he had already signed up to take a bunch of baseball players up on Eustis Ridge. There was a time most of the Yankee and Red Sox players got some off-season publicity by bagging a Maine deer. They came four at a time, and Flint usually guided them. Without a guide's license, he was heartsick. But he went onto Eustis Ridge with his ballplayers just the same, and when he led them through the woods he carried a big frying pan. Every fifteen or twenty paces he would bang the frying pan on a tree and shout: "I ain't guiding! I'm cooking! Don't need a license to cook!"

Game wardens were posted all around, hoping to nab this cook for some infraction, but it was true — you don't need a license to cook. It is not a crime to walk through the woods unarmed, banging a skillet on trees. Flint was eventually undone by much the same kind of equivocation. One of his ballplayers found a hunter, not in Flint's party, who had suffered a heart seizure. He was sitting against a tree in bad shape. Flint hove his frying pan aside, picked the hunter up in his great arms like a baby — rifle, lunch pouch, and all — and carried him at a trot to the highway. Here they found the hunter's automobile, and in the hunter's pocket they found its key. Flint laid the stricken hunter on the backseat and revved the vehicle down off the mountain toward first aid and a hospital. The hunter made a recovery and has been everlastingly grateful to Flint, but the wardens saw all this and they arrested Flint for "having a loaded gun in a car." It was the hunter's gun.

There was flak about this. Enough so the commissioner had to pay attention to it, and he wisely assigned the arresting officer to duty in a very far part of the state. And without fanfare, Flint found his guide's license had been restored. Too many folks felt enough was enough. Sort of makes me think of Cappy Dixon's "They didn't catch me fair."

There's one Flats Jackson story I haven't worked up yet, but I may. He was guiding an utter novice who was so completely inexperienced in the woods that Flats was nervous about him. Sometimes the greenhorn will spot a deer and begin spraying bullets around so it takes the fun out of the forenoon. So Flats said: "You sit on this stump and stay there, and I'll go down in the swamp and drive a deer up so you can shoot it. He'll likely come right up right about there."

Flats made a swing through the swamp, and things happened about as he predicted. All at once, from the direction of the stump, he heard rifle fire as if the Marine Corps was putting down an insurrection, and after a decent interval Flats came up the hill to see what it was all about. The hunter was still on the stump. But Flats had driven up seven deer and the hunter had shot all seven of them.

An inadvertence of this kind creates a problem. Flats had already tagged his own deer weeks earlier, so he couldn't claim one. The hunter could take only one home to Connecticut. So what to do with six residual deer was given a great deal of thought by the perplexed Flats. He decided, after considering everything, to go into the Christmas-tree business. The dressed-out deer, well secluded in the puckerbrush, quickly froze in the late-November weather, so spoilage was no problem. Flats didn't dare to take more than one carcass at a time, because that was quite enough to answer to if he chanced to tangle with a warden. So after he got his hunter headed off to Connecticut, Flats came with his pickup truck and harvested six loads of Christmas trees, hoping the nonresident landowner would keep his distance, and he brought each load home with a deer reasonably concealed inside. He was able to find six closemouthed friends who would admire to have a deer apiece, and everything came out fine except that the Christmas-tree market was glutted that year and he had to settle for a ridiculously low price. Hardly paid expenses.

I owe a great deal to Flint Johnson. Not just for his assistance with inspiration, but for countless experiences we have shared when Flats Jackson wasn't around. Such as the doughnuts he fried over an open fire at Eagle Lake. Such as his interminable tenor rendition of "You Had a Dream, Dear" the day we made twenty-two miles on Chamberlain Lake — it's the finest paddling music ever composed, and the rhythm suits both bow and stern. Such as a feed of trout below the dam at Spencer Deadwater. Such as the evening we plucked seventeen mallard ducks together. And such as the time we put out the big fire at Joe Pokum Bog. To name a few. That sort of thing goes with being a Maine author, and with a Flint Johnson in your stable you don't worry about things to write about.

6

THEN THERE WAS Del Bates. After a lifetime as camp clerk for the Great Northern Paper Company, Del retired to his native Patten, up in the shadow of Mount Katahdin, but he was ailing and didn't last long. I met him when he was boss of the cockshop at Scott Brook Camp, up beyond Seboomook, where he handled the payroll for over a hundred men and did the other paperwork required. Del described his wilderness by saying, "There is no law this side of Greenville, and no God beyond Seboomook!" He was wrong; Bill Dornbusch and I have found the presence of the Almighty a pantheistic axiom in Del's country, and every July when we come away we have prayed to Him in our manner that we may return.

When Bill's daughter married my son, Bill and I immediately anticipated becoming joint grandparents, a relationship that soon materialized, and we have called our fishing trip into the Maine wilderness each July the Grandfathers' Retreat. Sharing two grandsons is reason to rejoice, and there is no better place for rejoicing. The first year, before we were grandfathers, we pitched a tent at Baker Lake and whipped the headwaters of the Saint John River to a froth with our fly lines.

Bill and I are humble in our appreciation of a privilege. Baker Lake, and the woodlands for long miles around about, is on the other side of the chains. The private logging roads of the timberland owners are not always open to the public, and the passes we are issued each summer are recognized as corporate approval of our purposes. Except for canoeists, who don't need road passes, we see few people during our sojourn save the bosses and choppers, game and forestry wardens, and company men about their business. And the chain tenders, who look at our little piece of paper and lower the chains so we may pass into Paradise. About the second year we made our retreat we ran over to Pittston Farm, which was then a Great Northern operations depot, to pay our respects to Leo Thibodeau. Leo was employment man for Great Northern and one of the company men we could thank for being nice to us.

Leo came out of Aroostock County and spoke both French and English with a rolling tone only the

Acadians have — it is not at all like the diction of the Kaybeckers. After visiting Leo, pausing long enough for a noontime feed of prime beefsteak — Great Northern runs the best boardinghouses in the country — we said we hoped to find a few pan trout for breakfast. Leo tore a page from his pocket notebook, wrote briefly on it, handed it over, and said, "Give this to Adelard at Scott Brook — I think you'll find trout."

From Pittston Farm the company road runs the length of Seboomook Lake, crosses over Seboomook Dam, and sets a course past Beanpot Mountain for Caucomongomoc Landing and Baker Lake — also for Canada. We turned east where the fingerboard said SCOTT BROOK and left this road to find Adelard. It was fifteen miles to the chain at the camp, but this was an unattended chain and we let ourselves through. Up a short rise, and the first thing we saw as we came up was a huge flag the size of a double-bed sheet with the pirate design of skull and crossbones. It flew faintly in the meager July air, and from the location and the style of the camp it adorned we knew we had found the cockshop, or clerk's office. We had a note for Adelard, and we had no particular idea as to who Adelard might be.

Wilderness is wilderness, but the miles never impede the news. It's amazing how soon everybody in fifty square miles knows what happened when something happens. There were telephones then, miles of wires tied to trees, and now they have radios. Leo had cranked the woods line and told Scott Brook we were coming, so Scott Brook had been looking for us for three hours. The door of the skull-and-crossbones camp flung open and we first gazed upon Del Bates.

Del was built like a blue hubbard squash, with a plentiful belly that undoubtedly cost the Great Northern commissary a fortune. He called: "Welcome! Welcome, Gentlemen! Welcome to Scott Brook!" and he had a raspy, raucous voice like gravel in an amplified chute. He pumped our hands so our caps went sidewise and escorted us into his office, where two chairs stood ready for us. "Be with you in just one minute, gentlemen," he said.

Pleased as we were with the sobriquet "gentlemen," we were diverted from being smug about it by the appearance of the young man who was standing by Del's desk. He had come just a mite too close to a chainsaw and one hand indicated he had lost the bout. "Not too bad, not too bad," said Del, and he deftly applied disinfectant, gauze, and a bandage. The boy was a French-Canadian chopper who spoke no English, and when Del had him first-aided, the lad got in a pickup truck for a ride to the hospital in Saint Georges, Quebec. Then Del turned to us: "Well, gentlemen — what can I do for you?"

After that introduction to the duties of a camp clerk, I never asked Del just what his job called for, but we were impressed by the fact that whatever he did, a hospital in Canada was nearer than one in Maine. "I've got a note from Leo for Adelard," I said.

65

"That's right!" he barked. "Leo told me on the phone."

We still didn't know who Adelard was.

"Where're you stopping?" asked Del.

"We have a tent at Baker Lake."

"No fish up there. Fellow caught a chub in 1898 and they got it in the Smithsonian Institution. Nobody caught anything since."

I noticed that Del said "institution," another trifling distinction, but he was correct. He was not altogether correct, however, about angling in Saint John waters. Nothing was said for an hour about Adelard. Del had a Prentiss & Carlisle map on the wall, to which he had added some things they had missed, and he showed us the lay of the land. He pointed out Caucomongomoc Dam, ten miles east, and said, "I've got the keys to a camp there."

Then a pickup truck bounded into the camp clearing, braked in a cloud of dust, and Del said, "Here's Adelard, gentlemen!" In the years we knew him, he always called us gentlemen. Adelard descended from his cab, a medium-short French Canadian, a little stooped, his hands hanging in a manner that comes from long years with axes, saws, chains, pickpoles, cant hooks, and pickaroons. If you might see Adelard for the first time — his shape and his garb — on the Bowery, you might feel inclined to hand him a quarter. "Adelard," blatted Del. "Come meet these gentlemen!" We still didn't know who Adelard was.

He was the boss of the camp, the contractor who

managed the complete operation for Great Northern — hiring, firing, supervising. Del was the only company man in the camp. And the only native Mainer with English. Adelard knew a little English, but he was uneasy with it. I gave him Leo's note.

Leo's note was in French: *Do me the favor, good friend, to find our guests some trouts.* Adelard read it slowly, nodded, and said, "Bimebye."

So we sat in the cockshop and communed with Del Bates. Delmont Bates, of Patten. His father had been a walking boss; manager of several lumber camps, he walked from one to another. Of his three boys, he felt Del would make a good "pen-pusher," a camp clerk, so he sent Del to take bookkeeping and accounting at Bryant & Stratton in Boston. That his father was a good judge is substantiated by a remark Bun Bartley made one time. Bun is spruce-wood man for Great Northern, and he said, "If I had to set up a camp, and could have my pick of all the Great Northern clerks — it'd be Del." Del got a leave of absence the winter he represented Patten in the state legislature. As our years came and went and we saw Del each summer, Bill and I came to know that he was almost unreal. He had read libraries of books and seemed not to have forgotten anything he read. He would repeat whole poems — *Idylls of the King*, Wordsworth's sonnets, Holman Day rhymes — and he would toss off Shakespeare by the yard. His reading was no doubt to cheat the tedium of long woodland hours, but his passion for crossword puzzles could also do that — he never forgot a word. "Here's Adelard!" he said again, and we were about to go fishing.

Adelard (his last name was Gilbert — *zhil-BEAR*) soon scooted his pickup around the cookshack, drove maybe a mile, and stopped on a bridge. "Come," he said.

Leo knew. Adelard hustled us through waist-high puckerbrush, maybe fifty yards, to the edge of Withee Brook, and brought us out on a platform over the water. This was his private fishing pool, made comfortably available by the generosity of the resident sawyer — Scott Brook in those days had a sawmill. "Put de *mouche là*," said Adelard, pointing toward a mare's nest at the far end of the pool. We had *truites* for breakfast. And we had breakfast in the camp at Caucomongomoc Dam, for which Del Bates had the key. He also, he said, had the privilege of extending courtesies in the name of Great Northern. Bill and I have not used a tent since.

Del said his father was a stern man, but fair. He never dictated to the boys as to how early they should come home from Saturday-night pleasures, but he had a rule that the last boy in had to milk the cows Sunday morning. "We never knew how Father knew," said Del, "but whichever of us got home last was rousted out first, and Father never made a mistake."

Del told how his father took him into the woods to show him lumber-camp life, preparing him to be a clerk. "I was given odd chores to do, nothing important, but Father was teaching me the ropes. One night we slept at a camp, and there was just the one bunk for the both of us. I guess I had my little chores on my mind, and I was restless. I wanted to do things right to please Father, and I twisted and turned in my anxiety, and I gave him a bad night. It got pretty well along into the morning, and I was still rolling over and over, and Father gave me a nudge and said, 'Simmer down, Son.'

"Well, I was asleep, and with my little chores on my mind, so I roused enough to say, 'Yes, Father! Yes, Father — I'll take care of that first thing in the morning!'

"My father had had enough. He said, "The hell you will, chum — you'll take care of it right now!' and he kicked me out of bed. Spent the rest of the night on a chair. I thought daylight would never come. But the only reference Father ever made to this was at breakfast — he said: 'A good night's sleep is one of the most important things you can have. Leave things on your desk, and don't take 'em to bed with you.' "

Del said he got elected to the legislature because he was the only man in Patten who had a suit of clothes. His most delightful story, I'm sure, to a lot of good company men in lumber camps has to do with "the first order of business." Somebody down in the old Bangor office of Great Northern thought up something or other to improve efficiency and got out a general order, which went to all camps. Whatever it was, it was regarded as completely absurd by men in the woods who had better things to do. And, whatever it was, the general order said, "Please make this your first order of business."

Del got his copy when the mailbag arrived at Scott Brook from Pittston Farm, and he took due notice. He scoffed properly at the new idea, mulled it over, and then reached for the telephone. Ah! Those old woods lines! They hummed and crackled, using one wire and the ground, and the bulls of Bashan would have come across like the twittering of birds. Del rang Felix Fernald at Pittston Farm, and the two of them went into a yelling contest.

"Felix!" squawled Del. "You been at this game a lot longer than I have — what would you say is the first order of business in a lumber camp?"

Felix boomed back, "To get the man standing up to a tree so he can cut it down!"

"That's what I thought," said Del, and he hung up.

But to me, Del's best story was his private concert in Boston. The way he told it, I had little to do but remember his words and set them down. Here was this youngster fresh out of Patten High School, away from home for the first time, studying in Boston. He had to live frugally, and the lodging he found was some distance from Bryant & Stratton. He walked halfway across Boston to get to classes. And one afternoon he was returning to his room, books under his arm and a great deal of homework, and he crossed an overpass where railroad tracks ran beneath. Midway of the bridge, he heard a piano playing — completely out of context. It was lovely music, said Del, and "my first thought was, why aren't all these people pausing to listen?"

Nobody paid any attention. People were hurrying along, and Del indicated this was one trouble with city people; with this beautiful music in the air not one person gave it heed.

"I was disgusted," said Del. "I felt like stopping some of them and saying: 'Don't you hear that? It's beautiful! Stop and listen!' But I didn't. Anyway, I leaned over the railing on the bridge, and now I could hear the music better. It was real high-class piano playing, I could tell that, and whoever was doing it was no slouch. There was a railroad car down there on a track, and I surmised whoever was playing was in that car. So I looked around, and there was a stairway going down to the tracks, and I went down. Sure enough, this piano playing was coming out of the car, and now I could hear it plain as day, because the street noises didn't come down there. I sat on the steps of that car and did all my homework, and enjoyed a concert that went almost two hours. Lovely, lovely."

Del paused in his tale, tilting his head a mite as if still hearing some of the music. "Right in the middle of Boston, I was, and I had a piano concert all to myself. Turned out Paderewski was playing at Symphony Hall that night, and this was his private railroad car, and he played through his whole concert just for me!"

The way Del told it, I'm sure Paderewski never had a better audience.

When Bill and I go to Scott Brook now, one of our ceremonial duties is to lift a toast to the Old Pirate of the Cockshop. And it's not wholly because I miss his literary assistance.

7

RECALLING Flint Johnson, Cappy Dixon, and Del Bates, I despair of bringing Billy Edwards back to life to show his influence on my literary pose. Men like Billy come once. The things he did are not now important; the kind of town he lived in is gone; and the stories he generated are not now admired by the opinionated media that have replaced our newspapers.

In the 1920s and 1930s Billy was chief of police in Brunswick, and at the peak of his career I was just out of college, earning a whopping twenty-five dollars a week as reportorial staff of the *Record*. Billy was more than chief of police. He was also fire chief, first selectman, truant officer, bail commissioner, court crier, dog officer, deputy sheriff, humane agent, health officer, and a few minor things I have forgotten. There hadn't been a line-fence dispute in Brunswick for years, so the town was getting along without any fence viewers. But one day a dispute arose, so as first selectman Billy appointed himself fence viewer and settled the dispute.

In the *Record*, where Billy was involved in about eighty percent of the news, I tried to keep the proper hat on his head, and I always spelled him out — William B. Edwards. Nobody in town called him that — he was born there, grew up there, and was doomed to "Billy" forever. A truly mild person, devout as the son of a minister should be, honest in everything, thoughtful and kind, an enemy of strong drink, tobacco, and foul language, it was his lot to become the bogeyman — after he became chief of police mothers took his name in vain and would tell their naughty children, "If you don't behave, I'll call Billy Edwards!"

He was a short man, and so arranged that he could "strut sittin' down," except that Billy was modest and would hardly strut in spirit. He wore a uniform. The jacket was out of Keystone Kops, and his trousers never *looked* pressed. His faded cap had served him since he became chief, and lasted him until he stopped. There never was a man who looked less like an officer of the law, but there was never an officer of the law to outperform Billy. It's hard to believe that Brunswick, with a population of fifteen thousand, got along in those days with a one-man police force. Billy was it.

He had some help, I concede. For college commencement and football games, he had spare men to help with traffic, and he'd use them on serious cases. Mostly, he relied on Alexis J. Fournier, a French Canadian we called Dempsey because of a reasonable resemblance to the boxer. Dempsey was a mild-mannered and gentle brute who broke out his muscle only when Billy told him to, and when not on police duty Dempsey took movie tickets at the Cumberland Theater — a job requiring a natty uniform that would be a mite extreme for a White House guard. If an emergency arose during theater hours, Dempsey would go to assist Billy in his theater uniform. It was something like a peacock attending an ugly duckling.

Twice during my association with Billy, he proved the uniform doesn't matter. When Brunswick celebrated its bicentenary in 1938, the parade on Saturday was a magnificent turnout. One of the better "floats" was the original stagecoach that had made the run from Portland to Augusta, through Brunswick. Emery Booker had found it somewhere in fairly good shape and had had it restored. Six matched horses had been found to pull it — the same number as had brought the thing through town so many times so long ago. Emery and his lady, with a couple more in costume of the period, rode in the coach waving at the spectators. There was a man riding shotgun up front with the driver, and two outriders. Billy Edwards was one of these outriders.

He had a costume that made him look like a combination of Kit Carson, Daniel Boone, Bill Cody, and Sam Houston. Billy had an excellent collection of antique guns, worth a fortune, and he selected a brace of pearl-handled Colts to complete his ensemble. About a week before the parade itself, those concerned had the old coach out on the River Road for a dress rehearsal.

The advance rider, garbed about the same as Billy, must go incognito — I don't remember who he was — but Jesse Wilson, the road commissioner, handled the team of six. Emery and guests waved, and along behind came Billy Edwards on what Yankee Doodle called a slapping stallion. Just as this dress rehearsal got under way a Massachusetts motorist with a heavy foot ripped by in excess of the speed limits made and provided, so Billy hops off his horse, jumps into his Pontiac, gives chase, and apprehends. The tourist found it hard to believe Billy was the chief of police.

The other time was truly dramatic. The Daughters of Isabella staged an annual variety show in the town hall, all local talent, and one year while the Volstead Act was still in force, the show had a wonderful Thanksgiving tableau. The painting *The First Thanksgiving* was depicted with living characters. In the picture, you'll remember, some Indians are seen, with Captain Myles Standish, holding blunderbuss, keeping a wary eye on them. Billy Edwards was Myles

Standish, and the blunderbuss, again, was from his own collection. The curtain was to go up, revealing this tableau, and everybody was to stand like statues while a concealed chorus sang a hymn of thanksgiving. Everybody was on stage during the dress rehearsal when Billy got one of his tips.

Billy had quite an espionage system, and not much went on that he didn't know about fairly soon. On this occasion, Tapey Alexander came on stage during the rehearsal and whispered to Billy, Billy beckoned to the Indians (who were his reserve officers), and all hands left the stage. Tapey had whispered that a boatload of booze was being put ashore down at Mere Point. It turned out to be so. Taking advantage of Billy's histrionic involvement, the rumrunners had brought the boat right up to a wharf and were transferring the cans onto a truck. Supposing themselves reasonably secure, the rumrunners found themselves ignominiously arrested by Myles Standish and the Wampanoag Indians. The thing struck the rumrunners as comical, and they were all laughing when Billy marched them into the station to be booked.

Billy always had time to give me the whole background of any police work that made a story. I never heard him say "No comment" or tell me something had to be kept secret. He trusted me to keep faith, and I had the same trust in him. Once in a while he would suggest that tact, kindness, maybe judgment, should temper the way stories were handled, and as I grew in journalistic stature I found that he was always right.

Billy not only gave me stories, he taught me a great deal about how to write them.

The greatest single police achievement of Billy Edwards was his solving of the Cabot Mill robbery, which he did with my help. The Cabot was a cotton mill employing some eight hundred hands, and wages were paid in cash, each man's earnings in an envelope. Eddie Paiement was paymaster, and in those unenlightened days he simply went to the bank on payday and got a satchel of money. He had just returned to the mill office and was filling envelopes when the robbery hit him. Masked gunmen, and all that. When I heard about it I hustled over to the mill office, and Eddie was sitting on a stool, white as a sheet, trembling and fluttering, and babbling like a brook. Billy Edwards had already been there, but had disappeared within a few minutes. As far as I know Billy "investigated" this robbery with less than two minutes at the scene of the crime. I tried to find him later in the forenoon, but he couldn't be found.

By noon, Brunswick was full of constabulary. The state police moved in (in those days with numerous motorcycles) and so did the high sheriff with suite — a visitation from the high sheriff and suite was then a good bit like the ceremonial opening of a Grand Masonic Lodge. The FBI had been alerted. There was much scurrying about. Everybody in the Cabot Mill office had to be fingerprinted, and everything in the office had to be dusted for prints. There was great cry, and this was a major disturbance in peaceful little

Brunswick, where nothing like this had happened before.

I kept trying, but couldn't locate Billy Edwards. Then just before noon, he was on the telephone, and he said in a whisper, "Come to the pines on McKeen Road."

McKeen Street had houses for a way, and then tapered off into McKeen Road, which led into McKeen Woods. Scrub pine, mostly, and some blueberry land. The place was a lovers' lane by night and not much by day. I found Billy Edwards in his Pontiac and got into the front seat with him. Billy came directly to the point: he gave me one of these prison photographs of a man with a number hanging around his neck, and he asked, "How soon can you make me four hundred copies of this?"

I looked at it and said, "That's Red Griffin."

"Never mind who it is, I want four hundred copies as soon as you can make them."

"Be a good idea if I made an extra one for the *Record*, wouldn't it?"

"Yes, it would. But don't you print it until I tell you to. Now, how long does this take?"

Our little makeshift darkroom at the *Record* was not equipped for a job like this. I wasn't sure I had enough picture paper on hand. First, I had to copy the picture and make a negative, and it would take a while to dry. Billy said, "I want as many as I can have by half-past three." I knew what that meant — half-past three was our deadline for the westbound train to

Boston. Billy knew Red Griffin had robbed the Cabot Mill, and he knew he was in that direction.

I didn't finish the four hundred pictures that day. I had some by train time, worked most of the night, and finished up in the morning. Billy, under the McKeen pines, in extreme cloak-and-dagger context, said he now had enough photographs. The old sleuth filled me in on his progress. While the state police, high sheriff, and assorted trained seals had been milling around, Billy had circulated about town asking questions. Who had seen whom? Who had been around? Billy knew his town. He had his contacts. A couple of easy girls on a back street gave him his answer. Yes, Red Griffin had been in town. Red was local talent with a prison record, and somewhere along the line Billy had told him to shun Brunswick. Billy asked the girls if they knew where Red was now. No, but in idle chatter while busy with other things Red had said something about Rhode Island. Billy dug Red's picture from his file, gave it to me, and had mailed a copy to every police department in the Rhode Island, Massachusetts, and Connecticut junction area. Now we would just wait.

It put me in a bind. I knew something I couldn't print, but Billy hadn't done this for that reason. I had the only darkroom he could trust. During the next week the daily papers stumbled all around over Cabot Mill rumors, even to the point of risking apoplexy for poor Eddie Paiement by suggesting the robbery had been an inside job. I think I've never seen so much in print that said so little, but the robbery was important and the papers had to print something. That next Thursday we went to press with the smallest of all the stories about that robbery — we said there were no new developments but a reliable source indicated a solution soon.

I took one of the first copies off the press over to the police station; Billy read my story and said, "Thank you." And another week went by. Our absolute closing time for our weekly issue was one o'clock on Thursday afternoon. About half-past twelve the next Thursday, Billy was on my phone. "We got him," he said. "Picked him up this morning in Armstrong, Massachusetts. I don't have all the details, but I'm getting warrants to extradite Red Griffin and Scarface Williams. That's all there is right now."

The *Record* not only had a photograph of Red Griffin, but with great foresight — and complete reliance on Billy Edwards — I had risked the expense of a halftone engraving. In that way, Billy Edwards and I solved the Great Cabot Mill Robbery Case.

When the boys were arraigned in Brunswick Municipal Court before His Honor the Hanging Judge Joseph H. Rousseau, I spoke to Red Griffin. "Good to see you again," I said pleasantly, and Red said, "We shoulda known not to tangle with Billy Edwards."

That was one man's opinion. For my part, he was a great man in my life.

As a boy, forcibly attending church where his father preached in the Growstown section of Brunswick, Billy "signed the pledge." You should not, if I may analogize, make a boy swear never to kiss the girls, for many a juvenile oath of this sort evaporates in time. But Billy never wavered in his fidelity to abstinence, and in his last illness, when Dr. Earl Richardson suggested a shot of whiskey would ease his distress, Billy shook his head, and he died without knowing the taste of liquor. I wondered if this boyhood pledge accounted for his zeal in foiling rumrunners. No peace officer in Maine, including the Volstead Patrol, caught so many as he did. Yet in his zeal, he left one source uncorked, and unwittingly he kept a good part of Brunswick well supplied with booze in the times when it was hard to get.

Upon making a raid and a seizure, Billy had to transport the liquor to the police station, manifest it, seal it, and hold it for court's evidence. A half-century later, some people may find it hard to believe that from time to time, upon court order, officers would destroy this evidence by dumping it down a sewer. Trucks had not become huge in those times, and only a few people around Brunswick owned half-ton pickups. After a seizure, Billy would give a call to those who had pickups, and they would come to help him move the contraband. A caravan would thus arrive at the police station, with Billy in command.

There was always some deceit, however. When a truck was loaded and ready to start for the station, the driver would put a man up behind to guard the load, and it was the function of this guard not only to toss off a can now and then, but to remember where it landed in the bushes. Five or six cans out of every load would never get to town.

This contributed to the genteel life in Brunswick, but there was one man who prospered above the average. By faithfully aiding Billy Edwards in his transportation problems, this man set himself up as what he, himself, called "Official Bootlegger to the Students of Bowdoin College." His name should go on the institution's rolls of benefactors, of course, but the gentleman is now aged and infirm, and he might not like even belated fame. He may well be the only bootlegger Billy never heard about.

8

ONE BUBBLING SPRING of clear, crystal inspiration was dried up for me by competition. This gave me something to think about. Early in my Brunswick *Record* days I got acquainted with Frank, John, and Ben Coffin, brothers. They were perfect-pitch down-east, and outgoing. A short visit to one of them gave me material galore. I favored Frank, who didn't work quite so much at being a Coffin and could play the guitar to accompany his remarks. John and Ben had retail lobster stands across the road from each other at The Gurnet, and didn't speak. I never knew just what had set them against each other, but it was enough so their children respected it, and it took long years before some of the descendants acknowledged

84

some of the others. If I called on Ben, tact made me call on John, and I always respectfully alternated which one I called on first. On one of my earlier visits to John he told me the whale story.

John had what he called a "parcel of schoolteachers" out in his boat for some Sunday deep-sea lining, and as the cod and haddock began to come, a whale breached about seventy-five yards to port. Whales are common enough in outer Casco Bay during the summer months, but this added excitement to the outing and one of the schoolteachers took a picture. The picture showed the whale, and all the schoolteachers crowded to the port side of the boat for a good look. On the next breach, the whale came up so close to the boat that he looked like a cement wall in the second picture, and in the second picture the schoolteachers were over to starboard as far as they could get. John said, "I could have touched him with a short garff!"

John went on: "That's precisely the exact instant when I ups and says, 'Mr. Whale (sez I), that's *your* ocean! I want you to know that I don't want no part of it!' And I ups with my anchor and I gits!"

The yarn appeared in the *Record*, and I had further converse with Frank, Ben, and John for a couple of years. Then I learned that these brothers had another brother, Bob — sometimes Rob. I'd never heard of him. He'd gone to Bowdoin College, won a Rhodes Scholarship to Oxford, got to be a college professor, and owned a Pulitzer Prize for poetry. Now his proud alma mater was bringing him home to Brunswick to become an idealized homespun character in residence. They fixed him up with a professorship, and I became acquainted at once with Robert Peter Tristram Coffin.

When I said, in turn, to Frank, John, and Ben, "I didn't know you had a brother Bob," I got somewhat vaporish responses. Blood is thicker than water, of course, but there was definitely a reluctance to embrace this distinguished relative all the way. We have a way in Maine of withholding approbation without going on record. We say, "He's a helluva fine, all-right fellow, but . . ." We don't finish the sentence. I got something of that kind of approbation from Frank, John, and Ben. One of them went so far as to confide that Brother Bob had picked up the "Tristram" somewhere on perilous seas in faerylands forlorn, as it wasn't on his birth certificate. I found Rob Coffin to be a grand person; we became good friends, and until his early death (on a platform, reading his poetry at Westbrook College) he was a scintillating star in the Bowdoin faculty galaxy. But every time I saw him, I kept thinking of Frank, John, and Ben and their terminal "but . . ."

Robert Peter Tristram Coffin had been back in Brunswick only a short time when he turned out another book, this in prose, and as I also did all the *Record's* book reviews I read it at once. In it was my *Record* story of John, the parcel of schoolteachers, and the whale — just about word for word, and with nothing to indicate it had ever been printed before. I saw Rob soon, and told him I was pleased to see the whale story treasured up in a book — that I had always liked that "ups and gits" part. He told me in no uncertain language that *all* Coffin stories belonged to him, and he would thank me to remember that. So my source ran dry.

Many people, before I knew about Rob, had said, "Oh, you want to get next to those Coffin boys — they're full of stories!" So they were, but they had a brother to write them.

I suspect my wife of being slightly snide in her remark that was based on the drying-up of my spring. Robert P. T. Coffin (he was sometimes called Alphabet Coffin) brought out his *Book of Uncles,* an amusing and well-done series of essays about his own uncles, and when it was fresh off the press my wife packed it with her things when she went to the hospital to be delivered of our son John. She read it while waiting. A few weeks afterwards we were at a party, and she approached R.P.T. "Rob," she said, "I think you ought to know that I labored through your *Book of Uncles!*"

9

A PLENTIFUL BACKLOG of ancestors is a fine thing for a writer to have, and for literary purposes he will divide them into two groups. First are the real people. There were fourteen children in Jacob's family, one of them my grandfather, and Grandfather had eight children. My mother has various Scot, Irish, Dutch, and assorted derivations on file, and just about everybody in the Maritime Provinces is my cousin. In the Maritimes, an eighth or ninth cousin is fairly close. These are the real people, and family lore and legend are fair grist to an author.

Then there are the relatives one invents. These are

necessary because all true ancestors are pure and above reproach, and every family has a maiden aunt who worships genealogy. A writer can't go through life with her mad all the time, so when he discloses that maybe dear, sweet, grand-aunt Phyllis kept a brothel in Bangor, it is wise to allude to Phyllis under an assumed name. I learned this valuable lesson when I wanted to tell how my genealogy aunt wanted to join the Daughters of the American Revolution.

This is not all that hard to do. You prove that your ancestor fit at Bunker Hill or friz at Valley Forge, and enough records are extant so it's fairly easy. Anybody who was around in 1775 likely set up several lines, so sometimes an applicant can trace back in more than one way. But my little aunt, seeking the golden honor, ran into a snag.

It seems the Goulds were sometimes heroes, but had a tendency to be on the wrong side. A great many folks up in Maine had little taste for the American Revolution. We had one ancestor who fought for the Queen in Nova Scotia, and we had two that went to Quebec against Montcalm. This had set up a loyalist flavor, and we just didn't have anybody who was acquainted with Paul Revere and Ethan Allen. But my aunt persisted, and at family gatherings she would tell how her research was coming along.

We had another aunt, sister to my genealogy aunt, who was married to Bert Moore, a painter and decorator in Kittery. One day Uncle Bert was hearing the progress of the hunt for colonial heroes, and he said, "I suppose it doesn't help that I'm married to your sister?"

"No, that wouldn't help. It has to be in *my* line. Why, do *you* have a Revolutionary ancestor?"

"Oh, sure. Nobody ever looked him up, but we had one all right enough. Fought at Bunker Hill."

Curious, my genealogy aunt picked up the scent, and found in old records that Rutherford Buckley Moore, an early settler of Strawberrybank, had been a soldier and was the right age to have fought at Bunker Hill. The next time she saw Uncle Bert she said, "I've gone through the rosters of the companies that fought at Bunker Hill, but there is no Patriot by the name of Rutherford Buckley Moore."

"Patriot!" said Uncle Bert. "I never said he was a Patriot!"

Getting wounded on the way *up* Bunker Hill is no qualification for the DAR, and my genealogy aunt never relished being sister-in-law to a Tory. And this was absurd, because my Uncle Bert always thought the incident droll. I do, too, but the first time I used the story I invented an ancestor and spared my aunt a conniption fit.

We had an ancestor who showed Thoreau-tendencies before Thoreau. He lived at New Meadows, a fishing rendezvous from very early times, and one day he was thinking things over and said, "I don't go to church, why do I have to pay pew rent?" So he stopped paying pew rent. I found this in *The History of Bath.* They cited and censured the old boy three times for failure to pay pew rent. This was not only heresy; in those days it was extreme civil disobedience. It took a brave man, loaded with high principle, to buck the church and the state. I felt the old boy had the stuff, and I was proud of him. I thought our family was in good shape. But my genealogy aunt didn't agree. "Oh, dear," she said when I showed her the book.

Turned out she'd known about the old fellow's sins for years and had kept it quiet. "We don't speak about that," she said.

"Why not? They make a big hero out of Hank Thoreau, and he didn't tackle the church — all he tackled was the poll tax!"

"The two matters are very different," she said.

"How different?"

"Very different."

So the wicked sides of our family stories have always been saddled on fictional relatives. My aunt couldn't very well go about telling people that Mortimer Parsons in my story is really Tobias Coombs Gould, who robbed a bank. "Tobias," my aunt would say, "was a very successful man."

He sure was. He absconded with about a quarter of a million, picked up a redheaded schoolteacher, and went to Canada to commence a new career. He went west, where the Canadian Pacific Railroad was laying tracks toward the Pacific, and he redeemed payroll script at five percent. Five percent of the weekly payroll of Canadian Pacific sounds all right. He'd take the script to Montreal, collect at par, and hurry back out west to redeem some more script. The redheaded schoolteacher helped him. Before long he was a major stockholder in several Montreal banks, was able to contribute to numerous charities, and in due time made restitution to the bank back home that made all this possible. So much for Mortimer Parsons.

The best thing about invented relatives is that you can safely saddle on them all the stories you pick up about other people's relatives. I did that with William Goff. He was nobody to me, but he became so. Goff was an early settler of New Boston, Maine, and in 1775 got excited about the British in Boston. He walked down and arrived just in time to take part in the Concord-Lexington fracas. He was pumping reeking lead at the redcoats when an officer of one of the Massachusetts companies of militia noticed him and saw he was not in uniform. "What company are you with?" the officer shouted.

Bill shouted back, "I ain't with no company — I'm Bill Goff down from up in Maine, an' I'm fighting alone!"

Shortly I had a pleasant letter from somebody's genealogy aunt. "I'm sure your ancestor William Goff [she wrote] is my ancestor, too. I believe I am a great-great-granddaughter." Sorry about that. I had to tell her William Goff (who was a real person) never married, lived a recluse and celibate, consequently died childless.

There was another ancestor story I started with a quotation from *Abe Martin's Town Pump*. It began, "As Kin Hubbard once said . . ." I soon had a letter from an ancestry buff in Indiana who wrote: "I notice you have Hubbard kin, and I hope you can help me trace the parents of Clara Winslow Hubbard who came to Indiana from Biddeford, Maine, about 1830. She was . . ."

I wrote and told her all about Clara Winslow Hubbard. If I can make up my own ancestors, why not help other people, too?

10

WHEN Lester Markel was Sunday editor of *The New York Times*, he insisted that his magazine's articles have a "news peg." This gave me pause about a good deal of the piffle and trivia I was serving him from Maine, as it isn't often easy to find a news peg for yarns about man-eating trout or unplugged keyholes that let eight feet of snow into the front hall. For a good many of the veracities I invented I had to invent news pegs, too. There was one story I kept in mind for a great many years, for want of a news peg, and when the news peg for it turned up, it was my infernal luck that Lester Markel had retired. I had to find another magazine.

When agitation to convert the United States to the

metric system began, it was my news peg. We have curious ways in Maine to measure things — and how do you go about converting a smidgen to metrics? The idea gave good kilometerage. Nobody seems to know just how big, or how small, a smidgen is, but it is known to differ from a dollop, whisker, dab, dite, touch, flutter, and suggestion. The dite is the only one I could nail down. It was originally a Dutch coin of small value, a doit, and seafaring Mainers brought the altered word home to describe a trifling quantity. Just how trifling can be illustrated:

Two carpenters were moving a small building onto a new foundation, and one of them says, "Shove it my way a dite!" The other shoved, but shoved a little too hard.

"Nope — too much! I said a dite!"

Two dites might make a smidgen, and two smidgens a dab. A dab is just a little more mashed potatoes, please. But a dollop of mashed potatoes is a good slap of them. When a Maine conversation runs to these measuring words, it should be fun to hear a Rumanian translator converting to metrics.

I remember Mr. Dorrington, who was one of my Freeport people so helpful in a literary way. He was the best carpenter in town. He could rough out a henhouse, or he could do cabinetwork and gingerbread. He never used any kind of a measuring stick, but worked with an Alice-in-Wonderland system all his own. When he came to line up a job, he would squint all around and pick up a lath, or a similar strip of wood, and he would mark it off into sections with his dividers. There was no set length — he never knew what he had in feet and inches, or in meters and centimeters. He used this stick for that job, and on the next job he'd make a new stick. He used to make up words for his dimensions. He measured in pobbles, flummies, zoodicks, and things like that. He'd say, "Two jubbles and a thumb," and then saw off a board. Half the homes in Freeport were snug from Mr. Dorrington's handiwork, and he couldn't tell you the statutory size of any of them. I used to straighten nails for Mr. Dorrington, because I needed an excuse to hang around and learn things from him, and it never entered my boyish head that the day would come when he would have a news peg.

A whisker is the Maine refinement of a hairsbreadth, and a suggestion runs about that size. "Will you have some more gravy?" "Just a suggestion, please." If I know my Mainers, it will be a long time before anybody asks for half a milliliter of gravy.

What can metrics ever do for "the woman who weighs no more'n a straw hat, soakin' wet?" This not only conveys avoirdupois, in the Maine speech, but includes physical attractiveness — or rather the lack of both. That woman isn't the size of a barn door, and isn't beamy. You know that she's not built like a brick backhouse or a concrete battleship. What is the metric for two ax-handles across the shoulders?

Mainers still use Indian "looks" at times; the distance to the next house may be "two looks and a shout." An Indian walked to the farthest point he could see, and that was a look. Looks varied — from a hilltop you got long looks, but they shortened in a swamp. Kilometers seem inadequate for the wilderness trail. What about a hound-dog mile? A dog chases a rabbit until the dog drops dead, and that is a mile.

Years ago Ronnie Blake "went west." In some places that means he died, but in Maine, when the Prairie States were being opened up, it meant he went to the west'ard to seek his fortune. "Going out west" was like "going to sea." Ronnie went to Dakota and homesteaded. So his mother was telling about him and said her son Ronnie had gone out west.

Mary Blethen asked, "How far out west?"

"Well, I don't rightly know, but from what he writes, I'd say he's as far out west as it is from Boston out west."

"Gracious!" said Mary. "That's *some* far!"

Put that in metrics.

Gus Garcelon invited me to go to a benchrest shoot with him. Musket buffs were plentiful and they had a target range under a pall of smoke. I noticed the judges were measuring the target holes in metrics. They had some pretty close comparisons to make. One marksman brought in his target to be measured, and while he had all the holes in the black, they weren't bunched well enough to make him a winner. "I'm sure off today," he said, "I can't hit the broad side of a barn!" "The broad side of a barn" is standard Maine

jargon for poor shooting, and that's understandable —
but in this instance it amounted to a one-inch circle
(2.54 centimeters).

Maybe you remember the story about Mert Prindle
and Hosea Simmons and their hogs? Mert lived in
Harmony and Hosea lived in Cornville, and they both
came by chance on the same day in March to buy
baby pigs from Marty Fisher over in Wellington.
Marty sold them each a barrow out of the same litter,
and of course on that day the pigs were of a size. So
Mert said, "Tell you what, Hosea, I'll bet you a jug
that come Thanksgiving, my hog weighs more'n yourn
does!"

"Done!" said Hosea.

So the two plied their shoats well, and come
Thanksgiving Day Mert got his hog in a crate and
took it down to Skowhegan to the scales. It being a
holiday, the store was closed and the weights were
locked up inside, but the platform and the beam were
in the open, and Mert made do. He put a basket on
the beam, and his hog weighed two bricks, a peen
hammer, his jackknife, a plug of Everyday Smoke, and
a hen's egg. This balanced the pig, so he set out for
Cornville to compare notes with Hosea.

By the time they got Hosea's hog on some scales,
and had the basket on the beam, the hen's egg had got
broken. Mert kept Rhode Island Reds, and Hosea kept
Buff Orpingtons, so there was a reasonable doubt if
one egg was the same as another when it comes to
weighing hogs. The two gentlemen eventually had a

meeting of the minds, and Hosea lost. But there wouldn't be any story under the metric system, and under the Maine system, even though Hosea bought the jug, neither man ever knew just how much either hog weighed.

But I did find my news peg, finally.

11

CHOOSING THE RIGHT father is important in the pursuit of literature. Fathers are a dime a dozen in other pursuits, but few have the sustained understanding that nourishes the incipient author. I picked mine wisely, and after I had written a few books he admonished me gently about my self-esteem by writing one himself. After proving that anybody could do *that,* he sat around smugly suggesting that if I got too cocky he might just up and write another. In my years of growing up Dad brought me along so I've had many things to write about, with understanding of many things, and I realize his precepts and examples would stand me in good stead in any other occupation. I realize, too, that he gave me my good boyhood partly because he never had one.

He was born on the family farm on Lisbon Ridge in 1878, one of eight children to bless the brief union of Thomas Gould and Hannah Foster. Thomas had been a farm boy with four years in the first grade, and Hannah was a true lady from cultured Gray Corners with a diploma from high school. When my father was ten, his mother tired of the intellectual poverty of the old farm and walked out with seven of the children. Some have agreed that Hannah was too high-born a lady to continue in a situation so far beneath her. She should at least have had a piano, and a chance now and then to attend lectures. Myself, I've always wondered why it took her eight pregnancies to find she was so impoverished, but my father was always loyal to his parents equally and would give me no answer. He came home from school that afternoon to an empty house. He called for his mother, his father, his brothers and sisters — there were no answers. The sunken, all-gone, left-alone fright that moment gave him was to stay vivid in his memory all his life, and it had a great deal to do with the amiable conduct of our own home when he established it.

Dad found his father sitting in desolation on a box in the barn, staring at the wall, and his father said, "They're all gone, Frankie, all gone. Just you and me." Dad didn't like us to ask questions as to why the family broke up, but he never denied that he was always lonely in the growing-up, and he couldn't conceal the pain in his soul that his mother hadn't waited to say good-bye. Long before he had one, he vowed his home as an adult would have love and permanency.

Dad stayed with his father five years, helping with farm work, keeping house, and going to school. Such was the old subsistence farm, particularly that one, that there was never a healthy father-son rapport. After a day in the fields, they would both go to bed exhausted. In the winter, Dad would do his homework at the kitchen table, and his father would doze in the rocker over his *National Tribune*. Haymaking, cultivating, harvesting, and barn chores denied baseball, kite flying, and fishing. When Dad finished the one-room advantages of the Ridge School, his high-school classes were two miles away through the woods, and he carried a dinner bucket with food he had cooked himself. He didn't finish high school. He was fifteen when he "left home" — which means he set out to seek his fortune.

He found work on a dairy farm just outside Portsmouth, New Hampshire, and worked there until he shot the cat. The dairy barn had cats, and that's all right — a barn with cats is usually without rats. But nobody had controlled the surplus, and this barn had altogether too many cats. So Dad exterminated quite a few with a .22 rifle, getting the population down to a reasonable normal, and as he buried his quarry he noticed one had a pretty red ribbon. That afternoon the dairy owner's small daughter, about seven, came into the barn calling, "Fluffy, Fluffy, Fluffy!" That explained the ribbon.

So Dad got a job in a grocery store in Portsmouth, and went from there to the meat department of Houghton & Dutton in Boston. Next he became a conductor on the Boston Elevated Railway, running on the Brighton-Newton-Watertown cars out of Park Street subway station. He started on these runs at the Oak Street carbarns in Brighton, so he now gave up his room on Bowdoin Square and took lodgings in Brighton. That's how he met my mother.

Milo French, a Vermonter from Hartland Four Corners, was Dad's motorman, and his wife took boarders and roomers. Dad moved in. Milo's wife was from Prince Edward Island, and at the time Dad moved in she was entertaining her younger sister, Hilda. Dad was now twenty-seven years old, and until he saw Hilda he had gazed upon no female that seemed to penetrate the misogyny that stuck with him since he had come home from school that sad day. At nineteen, my mother out-Helened Helen and all the other measurable pulchritude available. Dad approached marriage in a practical way; he took a civil-service examination and applied for an appointment to the Railway Mail Service.

The marriage came sooner than planned. Another sister from "the Island," Nell, had also come "on to the Boston States" and was working in the Waltham Watch factory. She became ill, had major surgery, and as the time for her to leave the hospital neared, she needed a home to go to. Dad and Mother hunted up a minister, took a cheap flat up on Champney Street, and were ready for Nell. Everybody despaired of saving poor Nell, but she rallied under my mother's care, and lived to be something like ninety. She gave my father and mother a penny-pinching start on married life. But the Railway Mail Service was even worse.

As a conductor on the Elevated, Dad was too honest. Conductors didn't get paid much, as it was the Boston philosophy that a good conductor would steal enough to live on. Dad honestly cashed up every cent, until one day an inspector asked him if he had an independent income. He believed things would improve as soon as he was appointed to the Railway Mail. Not so. When the appointment came, it was as a "substitute clerk," and Dad worked only when a regular clerk was ill. When he was called to duty, the expenses involved usually exceeded what he was paid.

Grandfather, back on the farm, crated up a half-dozen hens and shipped them to Brighton. Zoning restrictions were far in the future, so a hen pen went up behind the house. By spring, Dad had hen manure, and he spaded a garden. He cadged neighbors' table scraps for his hens, and Mother sold cucumbers and tomatoes in the neighborhood. They made out, Nell was getting better, and then came his permanent appointment as a Railway Postal Clerk — a job he retired from thirty-two years later.

He worked in the Boston transfer office a time, and then went on the Vanceboro & Boston Railway Post Office, a job that shuttled Boston and Bangor. This meant he must move to Maine, as the job started in Portland, but he didn't make the move soon enough and all my life I have suffered the unspeakable indignity of being a native of Brighton, Massachusetts. I remember nothing of Brighton, but I remember everything after we moved to Freeport in 1918. By some miracle, Dad swung a big old ship-captain's house with an acre of land — big enough for hens, pigs, cow, gardens, berry bushes, fruit trees, and a mortgage that went on and on. But Dad was now secure in his work, with retirement benefits. His mail work was "six and eight" — in six days the mileage on the train accumulated the equivalent of fourteen days' work, so he got eight days off for what the Postal Service called "rest and study." Dad did study — as city clerk in the westbound crew he could recite thirty thousand Boston business addresses from memory — but those eight days at home were also well spent in his gardens and with his animals.

They were well spent with me, too. At ten, I was milking the cow and attending the hens. I hoed alongside him in the gardens. We cut firewood together. We played cribbage together. We explored trout brooks together, hunted rabbits and birds, and went for wild blackberries. He gave me my .22 rifle and took me to the woods to learn to use it. Somewhere along in those happy years I came to realize that Dad was bringing me so very, very much that his dad never brought him.

And in the house. We were four children now, and there was one rule the Medes and Persians wouldn't believe: *Mother* was boss! Mother was never austere. She was kind, loving, thoughtful, devoted, understanding, and so on and so on, but Dad still clung to his boyhood vow that the home would never get into any kind of a spin that would make for dissension. He had set up house in Brighton with the cheapest secondhand furniture he could buy (out of sheer poverty, because of Nell), but he had started payments on an upright piano and he found the money, somehow, for Hilda's piano lessons. By God, there was going to be culture in *his* house!

The postal work was hard. Dad was constantly thumbing his practice cards, studying route changes, train schedules, and new addresses, and I suppose he did as much studying as a physician. On the job, he also handled great bags and pouches of mail in a straightforward stevedore act — he developed a hernia in his first year as an RPC; indeed, the Postal Service considered hernias, varicose veins, and failing eyesight the incidental consequences of joining the Railway Mail. So his eight days off were properly earned, although most of his neighbors in Freeport thought he was lucky to have a job where he only worked half of the time. As the oldest of the children, I soon had the responsibility of the barn and yard chores when Dad was "on the road." There is no way to measure the value of such responsibility if one contemplates a literary career.

About the second summer in Freeport, Dad acquired a colony of bees. I was twelve. The things swarmed soon, while Dad was at work. He'd prepared an empty hive and had explained what to do, so I got into the veil and gloves and became an apiarist. When Dad got off the train at the end of his run, I was on the platform to tell him we had two colonies of bees, and since then I have been competent to write about bees whenever I felt like it.

As to the .22 rifle: Some of the boys I played with had Daisy air rifles, and I teased for one. Dad said no, and when Dad said no, that was it. But at Christmas I came down to find a single-shot .22 Winchester with my name on it. Dad said, "Air rifles are for boys." I shot rabbits for pies, crows in the sweet corn, rats in the henhouse, and now and then a pa'tridge that I caught sitting. Dad had every right to be ashamed of me the time I got the skunk, but he even made that an object of instruction. I shot a large and capable skunk with unerring accuracy right by the foundation of the house, under the pantry window. Mother got wind of this foolishness and upbraided me. The velocity of a .22 bullet is much slower than a skunk's dying curse, and until cold weather somewhat numbed the memory of that skunk she did all her pantry work in the parlor. Dad said, "Well, let's see . . ."

We tied a string on the skunk and washed him in the brook for a couple of days, rendering him fairly presentable, and then Dad showed me how to pelt him. We cured the hide, and in due time I sold it to a furrier. My skunk business was conducted at a distance after that, but every year I'd get a check from the Friend Hide & Fur Company. I've made a lot of money writing about skunks.

Dad had a ready wit, finest kind of humor, and he could tell a story — not always clean — with the best of them. His brother postal clerks liked to set him up for some kind of ludicrous consequence just to find out what would happen. All up and down the Vanceboro & Boston his remarks were quoted. One time a fledgling clerk was assigned to the crew, and he got on the train at Boston without knowing anybody in the mail car. He introduced himself, and everybody shook hands, and as the train howled up into Maine in the early night, the clerks set this stranger up for Dad — who would board the car at Portland. "You want to watch out for Frank Gould," they told the boy. "He's a bahstid!" They told the kid Dad was awful hard to get along with — cantankerous, surly, and all that sort of thing.

"Only one way to get next to him," they said. "He's nuts about poultry. If you can get him to talking about his hens, he might be friendly to you. But be careful how you handle him!" And so on.

Dad swung his satchel up into the mail car and

began to climb in. This new clerk, eager to make a good impression, gave Dad a hand to assist in the arrival, and he said, "Good evening, Mr. Gould! I'm Charlie Reffield, new clerk in the crew, how are your hens laying?"

Dad said, "Right through their anal apertures," and kept on coming. One of the other clerks in the crew told me long afterwards that Reffield was standoffish about Dad for a long time, and would eye him askance when Dad wasn't looking.

We children came to aid Dad with his studies. He had practice cards that represented Boston addresses, and a sorting case at home to work them in, and we'd hold them for him. This was his westbound job. On the eastbound train he worked Maine, New Brunswick, Nova Scotia, Prince Edward Island, and Quebec. So we children would read off a card that said, "Turnbuckle Street, 1 to 500." Dad would say, "Carrier route sixteen." If the key on the back of the card was "16," he knew that one and it could be laid aside. The ones he didn't know got further study. It wasn't long before we children knew the geography of New England and the Maritimes as well as Dad did, and this got me in my first schoolhouse bind.

Freeport had a landmark building (it's still there) called Codman Tavern. Commissioners of Maine and Massachusetts met there prior to 1820 to discuss the separation, and local tradition says the terms were settled in Freeport. Codman Tavern was chosen for the conference because it was on the stagecoach run from Boston to Bangor — which was the same run my father was now making in his mail car. Everybody making a trip down east spent a night at Codman Tavern. So in bringing this all to our attention, our schoolteacher asked us to come on the morrow with a list of the places the stagecoaches served between Boston and Freeport.

All my little classmates studied the "joggerfy" books and came to school the next day with their lists. Most of them had six or eight towns, some ten or fifteen. But the railway postal clerk's son was a smarty-pants — he came to class with a list of 387 towns, including those on the Rochester Division and the Portland & St. Johnsbury. I had set down from memory all the towns "pouched on" by Train 8 on the V.&B. R.P.O. No sweat whatever: Dad could go to the post-office building in Boston and "put up" his clerk's examination with a score of 98.7 percent correct; we children knew the cards about as well as he did.

My schoolteacher was not amused. She accused me of showing off, and was so exercised by my impertinence that she wrote a note to my mother suggesting corrective measures. Mother wanted to know what happened, and I told her.

"Where's your list?" said Mother.

I showed it to her. She looked it over and said, "You left out Arundel."

The didacticism involved is that sometimes a great deal of knowledge is a dangerous thing, and that moments arise when wisdom dictates prudence. I went on learning, even in school.

Dad always had doubts about the honesty of literary endeavor. That a week's pay could be derived from writing belittled his long hours at an arduous job. But his own lack of schooling in the cultural field made him ambitious for his children. He insisted we shun the secretarial studies and instead apply ourselves to the languages, history, and fine arts. In my instance, I'm sure he never considered that grinding Latin could amount to learning a trade. That three of his children became teachers was good; until he wrote his own book (*A Maine Man in the Making*, Harper, 1950), I think he was disappointed in my failure to measure up.

There was no motivation for his book other than to see if he could do it too. His mother, some years after the separation, had written a book. It was called *Feeding Babies* and it had many a homemade precept physicians could approve for fetching up healthy children. It was privately printed, and didn't sell, but it was a book. Then Dad's brother Ralph had written *Yankee Storekeeper* (Whittlesey House, 1946), which sold well. Lately a nephew, Ralph Moody (*Little Breeches*, and so on) started attracting attention in the book pages, and now his skunk-shooting son was on the bandwagon. Why not him? Dad paid five dollars for a flatbed Royal from the previous century, oiled it with gun grease, found a ribbon, and laid in some paper. He tried submitting one of his early chapters to *The Saturday Evening Post;* the editors used it as the lead article in the magazine. When his pile was big enough, Harper & Brothers thought it was no gamble at all. I submit that any author whose father is trying to show him up will work all the harder. Dad now had a new understanding of my efforts.

When a clerk retired from the Railway Mail Service, the other clerks passed the hat and bought him a red leather armchair. When Dad's arrived, he made Mother sit in it, and she liked it first-rate. Dad may have used it now and then, but he detested the inference behind it. He had a horror of "withering on the vine," and the last thing retirement meant to him was ease by the fireside. People who sat around reading western yarns didn't last long. Now he could give full time to his hens, his gardens, and his new grandchildren. When he was retired for many years, and had outlived all his old mail-car cronies, he was still grafting peach trees with an eye to the future. When he was in his eighties and he and Mother were alone in the big house, we tried to get him to consider a smaller place. "You're right," he said, "I should sell and find something better suited — but what would I do without my peach trees?"

Mother sold the place after he died. The night he left us, I threw some wood on the fireplace, took down his *Maine Man in the Making,* and read it again. On the flyleaf it says, "To John, whose example has resulted in this book's being written." Example be damned. I'd not have written much without my hand in his, without listening to things he said, without attention to his examples, without so much, so much, so much . . . The budding author will choose his father wisely. I was god-awful smart about that.

12

THE EDITOR of the Brunswick *Record* in 1924 was Robinson C. Tobey, and he was death on obituaries. I was halfway through high school then, just finishing Caesar's *Commentaries,* and the little lady who was writing the weekly page of Freeport gossip for the *Record* was the cause of Mr. Tobey's distaste. She had a morbid interest in death notices, and he couldn't seem to do a thing with her. Every week she would reach out all over the countryside and drag in several "late lamenteds" to sadden the issue, and from his desk in adjacent Brunswick Mr. Tobey didn't know if they were important to Freeport or not. Almost all her obituaries started with: "The community was greatly saddened Tuesday to learn of the

unexpected passing of . . ." The man might be ninety-
seven, but his passing was "unexpected." Survivors
were always "the bereaved." Mr. Tobey was ready for
a change, and so were the Freeport readers, and I thus
became a journalist.

When I wrote to Mr. Tobey, he assumed I was
mature and answered accordingly. He stated the case,
which amounted to his desire to get everybody into
the ground with as little space in the paper as possible, and he would pay me ten cents an inch. Now
"writing on a ribbon," which is what that kind of pay-
ment was called, is not good training. The tendency is
to let the words flow so the weekly check will be
bigger, but any tendency I had for that was thwarted
by the very terms of my engagement. I snapped
obituaries off in two paragraphs at the most, and in
purposely avoiding the little lady's kind of verbosity I
learned immediately that two succinct news items pay
just as much as one that is windbaggy. Mr. Tobey was
an excellent country weekly editor, and his occasional
approval of my items made me eager to please him
more.

All at once, however, Mr. Tobey and I struck a
snag. The years were passing for the storied sea captains of the glorious days of sail, and they began
dropping out just at the time I was cutting obituaries
to the bone. Freeport had as many deepwater sea captains as any town in Maine. Several had already been
"called aft" by the Supreme Architect of the Universe,
and I had covered them quickly with few words. Even

I, in my first few months of newspapering, knew that an era was coming to a close, and that we were hiking these old salts off to the churchyard without due journalistic attention. Behind every one of them was a full-column story that would dress up any publication. I spent thirty cents to ride the electric car to Brunswick and confer with my editor. Mr. Tobey looked at me and said, "My god, you're just a kid!"

He saw my point, and the obituary rule was relaxed. It was the very next week that Cap'n Brewer died. He was descended from the Master Brewer who built the *Dash* for the Porters. The *Dash* was one of the most successful Yankee privateers in the War of 1812, and after taking many rich prizes she disappeared at sea with a full crew of Freeporters. This gave rise to a "phantom ship" story, and John Greenleaf Whittier worked it into his poem, *The Dead Ship of Harpswell*. Why Whittier gave the *Dash* to Harpswell is unknown — she was Freeport all the way.

But the now deceased Cap'n Brewer had enough to go on without reaching back for his ancestors. He once ran a blockade out of Ceylon with a cargo of tea, and with a price on his head he never went back for more tea. On a voyage from Galveston to Liverpool, he had a crazy cook that kept a box of dynamite behind the stove in the galley. Whenever something irked him, he would grab up the box and run about the decks threatening to blow up the ship if "I ain't accorded more respect!" They cajoled the cook so he didn't explode, but it was a jittery voyage. They jumped him when they got to Liverpool, and the box really had dynamite in it.

Cap'n Brewer was also mixed up in the turkey story. A Maine mother sent a live turkey in a crate on a vessel that was sailing, to be delivered at sea to her son, who was master of another vessel. It was for Thanksgiving dinner. Connections failed — such were the manner of voyages — and the turkey made seven trips around the world before he was delivered. He was eaten, old and tough, in some such place as Hong Kong on the Fourth of July.

Mr. Tobey printed the entire story about Cap'n Brewer as written, as he should have, and a new pattern was set for certain Freeport obituaries. During the next ten years or so — and I still wrote the Freeport page — all the remaining old captains "filled to the north" and received full attention in the *Record*. I never called them "the late departed," and I shunned terms like *passed away, interment, officiated,* and many others.

There was a Cap'n Ward who saw the battleship *Maine* blown up in Havana harbor. He was ninety-two when the selectmen called on him to give him the Boston *Post* gold-headed cane, that newspaper's gift in its famous publicity stunt to honor the oldest man in every New England town. I sat by him during that afternoon and heard some of his stories — a macabre chore, because my interview with him on his birthday would be used later to help with his obituary. He sat in a rocker, the cane between his knees, and a planter of geraniums at one elbow. The room had that flavor of geraniums, kitty pans, tobacco smoke, salt pork, and fried smelts that I came to identify with old folks in Freeport. While Cap'n Ward talked to me, his wife kept coming to water the geraniums; they didn't need water — she wanted to listen. Cap'n Ward said, "Eyah, I see the *Maine* get it, full view — I was pickin' eyestones at the time!"

Cap'n Ward had nothing to do with Mr. Hearst's fight with Spain. At the moment of the *Maine*'s demolition, his nautical nationality was uncertain. He was on an English merchantman, with Norwegian papers — a prudent precaution considering the time and the place. He told me, "Every time I got to Cuba, I picked eyestones to bring home and sell, and there I was picking them up on the beach, when BAM!"

When Cap'n Ward died, I had all I needed to write him up, and I naturally included the eyestone — and this gave me a lesson in journalism of immense value. Nobody seemed to doubt that he had seen the *Maine* blown up, but nobody believed in eyestones. I did, because Cap'n Ward had shown me an apothecary's jar of them on his whatnot, some he'd gathered in Cuba but had never sold. You can look them up in the dictionary, which is probably the only place. They were some kind of small, smooth shell found on Cuban beaches, and when inserted under an eyelid they would "travel" and pick up a cinder or other irritating object. After finding the cinder, the eyestone would drop out. Drugstores kept them for sale, and even for rent. They were brought back by seamen such as Cap'n Ward.

The journalistic lesson was simply that reporters can artfully stir up readerships sometimes so letters to the editor pour in. Letters to editors are excellent copy, and even better are letters to editors that promote more letters to editors. We had a flood of mail about eyestones during the next few weeks, and Mr. Tobey wrote me another short note of approval.

When the controversy over eyestones was raging on the *Record*'s editorial page, Perley Meserve came into the office one morning and said he would like to place a small advertisement. Perley was an old-school apothecary in Brunswick, and until now had never placed any advertisements. He believed advertising suggested you needed business, and he refrained from creating such an impression. But today, he had something special. When the hullabaloo over eyestones began, he looked on a high shelf in his back room and found a jar of eyestones left over from long ago. Perley offered true Cuban eyestones at fifty cents. He told Mr. Tobey the original price had been a dime.

My very favorite sea captain was Cap'n Soule. I suspect Huguenot derivations, because in some places they call that *soo-LEE*. But in Freeport it was *sole*. Cap'n Julius Soule was the last blue-water man of the Freeport Soules, who built countless vessels at South Freeport and sailed them everywhere. He had married Edith Creech of "Hairpsill" (Harpswell) and during a long married life she always addressed her husband as

"Cap'n Soule, sir." He called her "the mate." I'd be sitting in his wide barn door milking him for stories, and she'd come from the kitchen and call, "Dinner's ready, Cap'n Soule, sir!"

There came a day when there were no more Freeport sea captains to send off. But their obituaries hadn't saddened the *Record*. Each had been a bright, happy vignette of a character who had crossed the divide. Biographies of a vanished breed. Years later, when I was writing for other papers, I heard some words of wisdom from Pat King, who was a writer for the Boston Sunday *Post*. A veteran, knowing his trade, Pat said: "No story is dead until you've sold it to the same editor three times." All those Freeport ship captains, and everybody else in Freeport, went up on my shelf for future consideration. Three times, Pat? When Cap'n Julius Soule, the last of them, came to the end of *his* book, my books were all up ahead.

13

BOTH Kenneth Roberts and Robert Peter Tristram Coffin opinionated in their books as to why Maine has so many more authors than any other state. Massachusetts has done well, but the Cambridge Poet was born in Portland, and Robert Peter Tristram Hawthorn got the idea of his *Seven Gables* from the Knox mansion at Thomaston. Pity. Roberts was cautious, but felt it might be the iodine. The surge of the ocean bruises rockweed on the Maine coast and releases wafts of iodine that swell the down-east lungs into literary enthusiasms. Coffin didn't discard this as a possibility, but felt the surest way to be a Maine author was to be born a Coffin on a saltwater farm at Pennellville with your lungs full of iodine.

Roberts listed all the Maine authors he could think of, and Coffin left out those not related to him and still had three pages.

One time there was a liquor violation case before the federal grand jury at Portland, and a witness kept telling about "neutral spirits." There was one pious-appearing juror from York County who looked as if he might be a retired Presbyterian preacher now devoting his time to writing Sunday-school quarterlies. Of all the good men and true, he looked like the best bet for a booze hater. But when the witness finished his testimony, this paragon of rectitude raised his hand and said, "If you please, I have a question — what is the difference between neutral spirits and grain alcohol?"

The witness gave a layman's answer, and this juror said, "Thank you, I've often wondered."

It was refreshing to gaze upon this gentleman, who looked so palpably abstemious, and picture him coasting along through the years reading labels on his bottles and wondering.

I've wondered about the plenitude of Maine authors.

Since earliest times, it is clear Maine has something that promotes literary endeavors. In 1556 André Thevet, already an established author in France, came to Maine to see what the place was like. His book is extant. His prose was stodgy and by no means outstanding until his vessel reached Penobscot Bay, and then he went into raptures and wrote beautifully. The same thing happened to James Rosier. He came in 1605 as scribe for the Weymouth explorations, and he'd never written anything much until he saw Monhegan Island. Then his words took flight. His job was to describe Maine so folks back home would get fired up and want to come over here and cut fish. He snared two boatloads in no time, which was good for the days before organized tourism.

In considering Maine authors in the aggregate, there's a problem. You can't always tell one when you see him. I remember a strange fellow who lived outside Brunswick. He lived alone in a big farmhouse, and nobody ever saw him except when he came into Brunswick on a bicycle to buy groceries and mail his manuscripts. He wore his hair long, affected an Australian campaign hat, and looked like a cultist who abhorred bathing. He wore a serape, or something on that style, with the corners tucked up in his pants pockets so they wouldn't engage the bike sprocket. Now and then children would taunt him. He was accounted queer, which in those days meant odd.

Nobody ever supposed he was a respectable Maine author, but he was. He had been graduated from Harvard Law School, summa cum laude, and had practiced in Baltimore for a few years with a deep desire to get away from it all and become a Thoreau up in Maine. Then a classmate had been named to the Supreme Court, and he was able to bring his desire to a fact. The classmate arranged so this fellow could do homework for him, and from his front room in the outskirts of Brunswick he wrote opinions for the United States Supreme Court. Would anybody remember the landmark decision that torpedoed FDR's NRA?

The difference between Maine authors and Maine characters has been considered. Holman Day, who wrote rhymes galore and numerous novels about Maine, later going to Hollywood to write scenarios for silent movies, left us one of the finest examples of classical unity. In one of his novels the entire action comes between the time the cookee in the lumber camp strikes the gong and the time the men sit down to eat. If you want unity, this is instantaneous transition. Aeschylus would have jumped up and down in delight.

But Holman Day was also a Maine character. When he worked for Frank Munsey's old Boston *Journal,* he was fighting booze. One day there was a big story, and City Editor Frank Lovering turned every available reporter loose on it. They had to find a certain man and interview him. Without this interview, there was no story. Press time approached, the city had been combed, and this man could not be found. Reporter after reporter came back, shrugging, and the deadline was at hand. Then Holman Day appeared, smiling and confident. He stepped through the door and said, "I found him! Got the interview! Everything's in hand, a hundred percent exclusive!"

Then Holman Day fell flat on his face in the dense fog of inebriation, and the office boy called a hack to take him home.

Not at all given to drink, Elijah Kellogg combined two jobs. His twenty-nine books came at intervals in his career as preacher at Harpswell, where he seems to have been a pious country character about whom somebody could have written a book. C. A. Stephens turned out miles of the old *Youth's Companion*, but was known around Norway (Maine) as a bit of an odd sort. Sarah Orne Jewett, Edna St. Vincent Millay, Edwin Arlington Robinson, H. W. Longfellow, Kenneth Roberts, R. P. T. Coffin, and Maine authors of that stripe, are spared close examination as Maine characters, but I happen to know Ken Roberts qualified with a number of folks in Kennebunkport. I remember a Bowdoin sophomore who said, "There goes R. P. T. Coffin again, imitating R. P. T. Coffin."

We must bear in mind a number of Maine characters who nurtured Maine authors: Edward Page Mitchell of Dana's *Sun;* Frank Munsey, with his empire of newspapers and magazines; James G. Blaine, the plumed knight and Augusta publisher; Seba Smith, who gave us *Uncle Sam* but was first of all a Portland publisher and seeker of talent. (Seba Smith's character Major Jack Downing was cartooned to become Uncle Sam.) A classic of American humor is Bill Nye's letter of acceptance when he was named postmaster at Laramie, Wyoming, but Bill Nye was first a newspaper publisher who had been born at Shirley, Maine.

I like the iodine theory. Not long ago *Yankee* magazine had a pretty little piece about cutting firewood. It was written by John Chase. *Yankee* identified Mr. Chase as the postmaster at North Edgecomb, Maine. Good place for iodine. Postmaster Chase had been sorting letters one day when the energy crisis was in focus; he knew about Maine woodlots, so he became an author. What iodine means, in this context, is the heritage and tradition of being a Mainer. We have a geography and a history that have led us into a way of thinking and speaking, and have made us articulate. From childhood, any Mainer is subjected to everyday language that Keats and Shakespeare and Milton achieved only after years of study and discipline. Bill Alexander, who had trouble writing and reading a grocery list, once said the potato bugs had ruined his vines. "They's all spars and no sails," said Bill. So there's no mystery about the origin of Longfellow's

A huge black hulk that was magnified
By its own reflection in the tide.

Longfellow just listened to a Bill Alexander. "Jim's walking for the Senate," said Harvey Briggs about a candidate who didn't have a whisper of a chance. "Frosty out" is what a Maine character says when it's forty below zero. The Maine author nods. Maine has its way of bringing authors along, and nobody is astonished when a fisherman's daughter (Ruth Moore) has a novel filmed in Hollywood, or a schoolmarm (Elisabeth Ogilvie) steps into the post office to mail a manuscript. Harold Jameson, my favorite lobsterman, paused to say howdy the other afternoon, and I said, "What're you going to be doing this evening?"

"Gawd, I dunno," said Harold. "I may go to bed, and I may write a book."

14

AT AN EARLY AGE I perceived a great truth
about food, and realized I had the right mother
to help me along. Mother was, and is, a cook without
peer, and she was strong on church without being
adamant as to persuasion. She told me once: "I don't
care what church you go to, and I don't care if
you don't go at all — but support one. Nobody's going
to like to live in a world without churches." In Freeport, she embraced the Congregational Society, but it
was a persuasion she knew nothing about in her girlhood on Prince Edward Island. Besides faithful attendance at morning services, she insisted that we
children shine up and attend Sunday school, and she
did her share in the subsidiary functions. One of her

activities was the Mizpah Class, and to support its charities this group of ladies held an annual fair. Mother was always "on the food table." This led my father to philosophize.

He said: "You use two dollars' worth of flour and sugar and eggs and whatnot, and donate a cake to the fair that takes you all morning to bake with my fire-wood, and then you sell it for fifty cents for the Glory of the Lord. Then you pay fifty cents for a cake some other woman baked, and it isn't worth a quarter, and you bring it home and make me eat it. I'da damnsight rather eat your cake and give the foolish Mizpah Class five dollars!"

Mother said, "Oh, Frank . . ."

I realized from this that my mother baked cakes that appraised at five dollars, and that's a good kind of table to sit at.

When Mother and Dad went to housekeeping in Brighton, Massachusetts, they were poor as swale grass. It is likely true that the handful of laying hens and the little garden kept them from going hungry while the Postal Service was delaying his appoint-ment. And somehow, as Mother sold eggs in the neighborhood for ten cents a dozen, or let cucumbers go at a cent apiece, she managed to put by a penny here and a penny there which, unbeknownst to Dad, she salted away in a cream pitcher in the cupboard. It is incredible that in time she would have change enough to make the difference in the family finances. As long as she kept house, Mother had her pitcher on the shelf. Afterwards, in Freeport, she was able to save coins larger than pennies and nickels. We children never counted on it, and neither did Dad, but time and again she would fetch the pitcher down and find the price of a new necktie or a new hair ribbon, and more than once enough to make up the mortgage money.

I must tell about her shoes. Mother had — has — a long, narrow foot that a great many shoe stores were never able to fit. There isn't a foot like hers on the next million women. To spare my father the great expense of special prices for special shoes, Mother discovered during the Brighton days a great benefactor known as Filene's. Filene's is a department store in Boston, and long ago it invented a sales stunt which it called the Automatic Bargain Basement. Goods in the store upstairs that did not move on schedule were taken to the basement and sold at sale prices. Then for a month the prices were automatically reduced periodically, and if at the end of the month an item had not been sold, the store gave it to charity.

Shoes, when turned out by a factory for wholesale purposes, are made by the thousands of pairs — from little to big, all widths — averaged out so the greatest number of pairs is in the range of the greatest number of expected sales. Filene's would sell shoes hand over fist, but nobody except Mother ever came in for the long, narrow size that she could wear. It occurred to her that if she didn't buy her shoes upstairs at the fancy price, they would soon be in the basement. And since nobody else in Greater Boston was about to buy her size of shoe, all she had to do was wait for the last automatic-markdown day of the month, and just before the shoes were donated to charity she'd buy all that Filene's had for ten cents a pair.

Any presumption that Mother was Scotch is reasonable; she was descended from "The Norman" — Norman MacLeod, who came to Prince Edward Island in the first wave of Gaelic immigrants from the Isle of Skye. The clannishness of the Highlands was intensified on the red soil of that small island in the Gulf of Saint Lawrence, and today at least half the people in the province are my relatives. As well as all the MacLeods, anywhere. Mother's childhood was as bucolic as Dad's, but with a happy home. The farm produced nearly all they had, and the trick in the kitchen was to take what they had and make it nourishing and palatable. Of Grandfather's seven children, only one — Sam — was a boy. Sam had taken off for the Klondike when he was nineteen, and by driving four stakes into that rich land he had made himself wealthy. This left only girls at home, plus Grandmother and a maiden aunt; my mother's training for housekeeping was distaff-oriented. After we were established in Freeport, things were prosperous enough so Mother could take us children and go to "the Island" every second summer or so to visit her parents, and I came to know well her girlhood farm.

Once we went on one of the white Eastern Steamship vessels — the *Calvin Austin,* by way of Saint

John (and that's a memory to have in your bank) —
but mostly we went by train. It would be my father's
train, and sometimes he was in the mail car up ahead
as far as Bangor. Then we'd ride on to Sackville and
change to a smaller train for the ferry and the Island.
There is only one Island. Anne of Green Gables said it
is the prettiest place in the world, and it may well be
with its red soil and green trees, its lush fields and
its share of the ocean. When Colin MacKay (undoubtedly a cousin of mine) went from the Island to
"the Boston States," he told them he came from the
Island, and they said, "Which island is that?"

Colin spoke wisdom and said, "P.E. Island — what
other island be there?" When the ferry pulls out from
Tormentine, New Brunswick, and the visitor sees the
red shore of P.E.I. rising from the sea, he will share to
some extent the leaping of the heart that welcomes all
Islanders home when they have been away. My
mother would choke, squeeze our hands; and we came
to know how she felt. Except when I've been home,
my happiest times have been on the old farm near
Vernon River, P.E.I. Mother would race through the
fields with us, catching up her skirt to clear fences,
and she'd take us to special places like Finnegan's
Brook and the Hermitage school.

I sat at the bench where my mother sat in the
Hermitage school. One room, quite by itself in the
landscape, it was right out of "The Old Oaken
Bucket," and Mother walked nearly a mile through

the woods to reach it. She told us how she'd wait in the morning for the Ross children, who had to walk nearly two miles. She'd hear them coming up the lane — the farm lane, not a public way — singing "Red River Valley" as they walked, and Mother would run out to join them, singing. When the snow was deep, the older Ross boys would break a path, and one of them would carry their little sister. "This is where *I* went to school!" she said, and hugged me as I sat at her bench with her.

Years later I was in college and I met up with the Lake Poets, and one Sunday when I was home for dinner I said something about Wordsworth. Mother put down the teapot at her end of the table, cocked her head in a remembering gesture, and without a hitch repeated *Ode: Intimations of Immortality from Recollections of Early Childhood.* If you haven't looked at it lately, it runs to about eight pages of text in any anthology. We children, and Dad, sat spellbound. "I had to learn that in school," Mother said. The literary gems she read, and memorized, at the Hermitage school would have passed her in any English-major exam, and I know because I passed one.

When Mother came to have her own home, her training in the Island kitchen proved ideal. She was anything but well-to-do, but we children ate like millionaires. The only time my mother bought a loaf of store bread was when she needed a stale loaf. She'd send me to the market for a loaf of stale bread, and

Mr. Magoun would nod and say, "Stuffin' a chicken, eh?" Otherwise she baked four loaves on Wednesdays and four more on Saturdays.

During World War I, a big, fat general all bowed down with the responsibility of gold braid came to my school to give us a win-the-war pep talk. We saluted the flag and sang "America," and then he recited his memorized harangue. He wrote a recipe for "war bread" on the blackboard, and we little patriots were to copy it off, take it home, and urge our mothers to use it — it was nutritious, it was cheap, and it would help win the war.

Mother looked my paper over, said I had misspelled a word here and there and should be more careful, and agreed to try it. The next Saturday she baked four loaves of the general's bread. It was good, but not so good as my mother's, and my mother scribbled on a piece of paper and said the general's bread cost forty-seven cents a batch more than hers did. At our house, we finally won the war on Mother's bread.

Being a farm girl, Mother was at home with Dad's hens, gardens, and cow — but not with the bees. Bees never liked my mother, and if she stepped out to hang a dishcloth on the piazza line one would like-as-not nail her from afar. When Dad and I took off honey, which stirs bees up, she'd go in the pantry and shut the door — covering her timidity with the excuse that she was making buttermilk biscuits. When the danger was by, she'd come out with a pan of biscuits ready to pop in the oven — and buttermilk biscuits are the tare to new honey's tret. Had my mother no other merits, she would still be the greatest because of her butter-milk biscuits. She canned and preserved, helped pick in the gardens, and when necessary would milk the cow. She refused to dress out a hen, but I'm sure she could have. Dad was a sociable sort, and often invited waifs and strays, on the spur of a moment, to stay for dinner or supper. Mother would thus occasionally find she suddenly had four more at table, but she always fed them.

Only once did she demur. Dad had hired Manley Higgins and Curley Daigle to come with a hand suc-tion-pump and clean out our cesspool. Redolent from this task, they were invited to dinner. Mother had been watching these worthies through the window, and she said nothing doing. She put her foot down. Dad said, "But I've already asked them!"

Mother said, "Well, un-ask them! I will not have those stinking men at my table!"

So Dad drew some pails of warm water, laid a board over two barrels behind the barn, and super-vised the nettoyage of Manley and Curley, bringing them to the house shining like bottles. Mother fed them and sat smug, as if she'd not only made a point but wrought a miracle.

I have no idea why Mother skipped a blessing at meals. It was usual in her childhood home, and she had taught us children our evening prayers — up to a reasonable point she insisted on hearing us repeat them. She leaned religiously, always. But she never said a grace at table, and I don't remember she ever called for one. At her table, thanks were understood and automatic, and Dad substantiated this one time by saying, "If God doesn't know already how we feel, He's not living up to His advertising." On special occasions, or out of deference to a special guest, Dad would sometimes ask for a blessing. Once we had a minister with us, and Dad asked him to "say a few words."

"Oh, no," he said, "I believe it is better for the man of the house to do that!" We children, and Mother, stared pop-eyed as Dad fell to without a hitch and asked one of the finest blessings ever offered. Afterwards, once in a while, we children would tease him to do it again, and he'd say, "Go ahead and eat!" At Thanksgiving and Christmas, when we had family crowds, Dad would ask his maiden sister to give the blessing. She would, and she always dwelt on our togetherness and the joys of family ties. This had a special, poignant meaning to the children of Thomas and Hannah, and when they lifted their eyes my aunt and my father would look at each other in an esoteric way. I came to notice that Mother would tactfully break the tension of these moments by handing my aunt the butter, or something.

Mother was always "scairt to death" at riding in an automobile. Even today, she will hang on to a door latch on curves. My father was perhaps the worst highway menace since wheels were invented, but Mother always rode with him in composure. Our first automobile was a 1917 Model T Ford, which Dad bought from a fellow postal clerk for a hundred dollars. The man left it in the dooryard one day while Dad was at work, and when he came home he got his license and plates, and set out to learn to drive. He didn't know about retarding the spark, so when he cranked it the contraption jumped about a foot in the air and shook like a baby's rattle. Dad quieted the thing with many a "So, so now!" and without knowing the least thing about automobiles he belted out of the dooryard like a hound on scent and was gone for three hours.

For years the outskirts of Freeport remembered that afternoon as an occasion for prayer. Dad chased dogs on their own lawns, frightened woodpiles, splashed washings on lines, and caused horses to elope. He backed and filled at every crossroads ("Gettin' the hang of backin' 'round") and when he came home he had the Ford tamed. He eased off the throttle by our back steps and called, "Come on, Hilda, I'll give you a ride!"

None of us children would have gone near that Ford unless whipped, but Mother tied on a hat, walked over calmly, climbed in, folded her hands, and looked (although she was prettier) like Queen Victoria awaiting Disraeli. Dad made a turn around an apple tree, missed the rain barrel, and found the highway. We children may have thought we'd never see either alive again, but if it had been Mother's lot to perish that afternoon, our last recollection would have been fitting: serene, confident, happy, possessive, very much in love, and beautiful. She wouldn't let Dad drive out very far that time, because she had to get home and start supper.

15

ANY EXEGESIS meant to explain authoring or bring advice to those "interested in writing" should have a few words about editors. For the most part, they are a great help, but there are odd ones. They are, however, a lot like the Supreme Court, which is right even when wrong, and the editor who proves odd should be respected and forgotten. Find another one.

There were a few times I felt my editor had not measured up.

My father told me the story of the well up the road that stayed flowing when all the other wells in the vicinity went dry in a drought. Farmers asked the owner of this well if they might bring their cattle around for a drink, but he was arrogantly possessive and said no. Things got worse, and water was hauled in barrels for miles, but this fellow with the one good well refused to share. One day a couple of boys were walking by and they saw this fellow up on the roof of his barn repairing shingles, and they took the ladder down. There he was, and he sat up on the roof yelling his head off while the whole community drove horses, cows, and sheep up to his well and pumped them their fill. After all the animals had had a good drink, somebody put the ladder back and ran for it.

I'd been working on this yarn, trying to bring it into shape, and I got an unexpected letter from an editor on *Farm Journal*. *Farm Journal* is still being published, but with a new batch of editors — which may be just as well. This editor said he'd been watching my articles in the Sunday magazine of *The New York Times*, and he thought their farm flavor would go very well in *Farm Journal*. If I had anything for him, he would like to see it. So I sent him the yarn about the farmer who wouldn't let his neighbors use his well.

He sent the piece right back, saying it wasn't just what he had in mind, but if I had something else another time, he'd like to hear from me again. So I sent the story about the well to *The New York Times* and a couple of months later it appeared in the magazine, and I got the usual complimentary letter from Lester Markel: "Orchids to you for a fine piece . . ."

About a week later I got another letter from this

editor on *Farm Journal*. He enclosed a clipping of the well story from the *Times* magazine, and he wrote: "This is more in line with what we hoped to have from you."

I've never tried to figure it out, being willing to grant that some editors are odd, but perhaps the incident explains why *Farm Journal* is one of the few magazines whose pages I have never graced. Pity — it's a good publication.

One of my strangest experiences with editors was with a dearly beloved editor on *The Atlantic Monthly*, Charles Morton. He had used an occasional piece of mine, and I was always looking for another to send him. One day the State of Maine was shocked by a most brutal murder. A couple of hitchhikers had come up from Massachusetts and had wantonly done in an elderly recluse. For some reason that was never elucidated, the police and the courts showed reluctance to get busy about this, and in the end the two culprits were put on probation on condition they leave Maine. An editorial in the Lewiston *Journal* tongue-in-cheeked that perhaps the court was lenient on the grounds that our tourism would suffer if word got out that we were tough on visitors.

The piece I sent to Charles Morton was titled *Murder in Maine*. It differentiated between manslaughter and involuntary suicide, and it had one line that went: "Police seldom enter a case unless the Boston newspapers want pictures." It was satire, and it wasn't that bad. Editor Morton saw the wit in it, was delighted, and sent me a good letter with a good check. I spent the money.

Quite a while later Editor Morton sent the manuscript back to me with a most apologetic letter, saying that the legal department had a few qualms about printing the thing, and rather than take a chance he decided to skip the piece. Sorry, and so on, and if you have something else I would like to see it. I didn't return the money, and he didn't ask for it.

Well, about two years went by, and Mr. Morton wrote to me again. He, in particular, and some of the other editors as well, remembered the *Murder in Maine* piece with great pleasure, and from time to time they conceded it should have been printed. Would I be good enough to let them look at it again? I mailed it to *Atlantic Monthly* a second time, and got it back a second time — and with a second check. It made three trips in all, and *Atlantic Monthly* never did print it. It is the only manuscript I ever sold three times to the same editor without it's being published at least once.

From a literary point of view, I would guess that the poorest person in the world to pass judgment on a satire of the judicial system would be an attorney working for a publisher, and I have never held Mr. Morton to blame for his triple rejection. Otherwise, until he died, he and I had a good relationship.

A mirthful rejection came from Hugh Gray, who

was editor of *Field & Stream*. We had a total eclipse of the sun one year, which cast a shadow up across northwestern Maine into Quebec. It came about noon on a summer day, and I happened to be visiting Buddie Russell at Kennebago Lake — right in the path of the eclipse. The evening before, we were talking about the eclipse and somebody said the birds go to roost and all nature reacts as if 'twere twilight. I said: "Why don't we do a scientific study and find out how the landlocked salmon react to an eclipse? Tell how to catch salmon while the sun is blacked out. There isn't going to be another eclipse for four hundred years, and it might strike somebody funny."

Buddie, Gibber Philbrick, and I accordingly went down the lake the next morning, lunches packed, and walked down Kennebago River to Canoe Pool. Here we set up our "scientific expedition," and made notes on the progress of the eclipse. It was true: as the shadow grew, birds twittered and went into the trees; frogs croaked as at twilight; the breeze stirred, as if at eventide. Now we needed to know if salmon, usually inactive at midday, would begin to take flies as they do at dusk. And so on. I took pictures, and Buddie took a salmon. Just like twilight.

Hugh Gray returned the piece to me in the next mail, and his letter said, "Since we won't have another eclipse for 400 years, I think we must pass this story up."

I showed the rejection letter to Buddie Russell, and

Buddie said, "Why the hell does he think you wrote the piece?"

I don't know. But sometimes editors may be odd, for whatever reasons, and I've decided not to do anything about it.

16

THE PROPER Maine author derives his greatest support from the Maine schoolteacher. Along in March and April the high schools come to that scintillating part of the English classes known as "Maine Authors." Those of us belonging even loosely to this fraternity begin to get letters in the mail, and they'll come by sevens and tens in every mail for about two weeks. This one originated in one of our larger high schools:

> Dear sir:
>
> We are studying Maine Authors in our English class and my teacher, Miss

Shingle Dingle, has assigned me to write your autobiography. Will you please send me all information like when you were born and what you have written, and what your books are all about. I have to turn this paper in next Tuesday, so you don't have much time.

Yours Trueley,

——— ———

I have disguised Miss Shingle Dingle. There was no postage for reply.

One must not get mad at the youngsters, but it would be fun to take a baseball bat and chase a few Miss Shingle Dingles seven times around the curriculum. At least the teachers might suggest return postage. Unless I am all drove up with something else, I try to answer these letters — I feel it isn't the pupils' fault and I shouldn't take my mad out on them. I answered this boy. I suggested he read my books to find out what they were all about, and told him to consult *Who's Who* to find out about me. And I said that if he really didn't mind, I would prefer — truly — to write my autobiography myself.

So why didn't his teacher tell him all that? Presumably the purpose of the study is to collect information, learn to evaluate it, and produce a composition — in which situation he doesn't have to write about me. Instruction would be just as effective if he took Zane Gray, Thomas Carlyle, or even Smokey

Burch, who sells alewives in the spring (but not very many).

About a week later I got this letter:

> Dear Mr. Gould,
>
> I think it is only right that I tell you how very disappointed —— ——— was that you didn't send him the material he requested. He has been a great fan of yours and had his heart set on writing your autobiography. I think you ought to know how badly you let him down.
>
> (Miss) Shingle Dingle

I should, I suppose, have helped him with my autobiography, but I'm still dubious about a "great fan" who didn't know what my books were about.

If the alleged educational system would tackle this in a saner way, I would be most happy to cooperate my heart out. It is truly pleasant to sit with a young person who is "interested in writing" and encourage him/her. I was watching a Bruins-Canadiens hockey game one evening on television when my telephone rang. The game was tight and I had a cordial to help me along, and I had not cark nor care. I set out not to answer. But I did, and a girl's voice was trembling and unready. Sounded like Father Mahailovitch when he dreamed he was confessing his sins to God — "scairt like hell." But the girl came into gear and said she was writing a paper about me for English, and she wondered if I might have time to talk to her.

"Sure thing — when do you want to come?"

"You mean I can come?"

"Of course. Anytime. Can you come now?"

I never knew how that hockey game came out. She was indeed like Father Mahailovitch, but one of my homemade root beers got her at ease soon and made an excuse for me to keep on with my cordial. She said her teacher had told her to write me, but her father thought that was the wrong thing to do. "Go over and see him," he said, although his taxes will never be reduced for this wise assistance to the school department. The girl got an A-plus on her paper and brought it around to show me. If she'd got less than that, I might have gone gunning for that teacher.

Another young lady showed me a paper one time that an "English teacher" had corrected. The theme started off:

> The place of leaving was the sunrise shore of Mountain Lake, and as we made the boat ready we could barely see, through the mists of the morning over the water, the buck deer staring at us from the sand bar at the mouth of the cove.

This teacher had corrected "place of leaving" to "point of departure." So much for some English teachers.

I had some fine English teachers, and know I was lucky, but they were like Democrats in Freeport. When my sister Kathryn went to Bates College, she took a course in political science, and one day in a lecture the professor said something about the Democrats. My sister responded like any all-Freeport Republican, and to reprimand her the professor said, "What's the matter, Miss Gould — don't you have Democrats in your wonderful little city of Freeport?"

Kathryn said, "Oh, yes, sir — there's Guy Bean, Elmer Porter, and Ben Stilkey."

Good teachers, from kindergarten to a degree, can often be counted on fingers. One of my great teachers was Thomas Means, and his superiority may be demonstrated by the way he introduced us to Homer. We came into the first class, he discharged the amenities like a shorted battery, and he said: "Gentlemen — It would probably cause talk if the young ladies of the community came to the gymnasium after a football game and bathed the athletes. But in ancient times, it was customary for the handmaidens to wash a gentleman after a hunt, games, or a battle. For next class, I want you to be ready to cite instances of this in the *Iliad*. If you will count off, you will have the numbers of the books each man is to explore. Good day."

At our age, at that time, in a conservative college, there was a bawdiness to this that resulted in no "unprepareds" the next time. And in succeeding classes Professor Means had us look for similar things — until each of us had read all the books and knew all the *Iliad*. Which is an excellent thing for a writer to know.

Thomas Means was a classical positivist, and wouldn't say "Good morning" unless the sun was out. It amused a lot of us when he got hung up, in after-years, on a bit of Latin. The Maine legislature passed a law about propagating shellfish, and it said that upon application the municipal officers "shall" issue a shell-fish license. When the Brunswick selectmen refused to issue him a license, Professor Means rallied, and demanded that they do so. "The law says 'shall,'" he pointed out. "You have no discretionary powers. Issue the license or I'll go to court!"

This foolishness actually got into the Maine Law Court, which is our supreme judicial body, with Professor Means carrying the torch for composition and rhetoric, and also picking up the legal fees. But great as he was as a student of Latin and Greek, the matter had a wrong case ending.

The justices could have stabilized syntax and cleared up the whole grammatic issue of *shall* and *will, may* and *must*. But in legal dignity they ducked the issue. They decided that Professor Means had appealed his case on a mandamus, whereas he should have proceeded under certiorari. They threw the thing out. In class the next day Professor Means digressed beautifully about *shall* and *will,* the stupidity of the courts, and the IQ of legislators who fancy they can write — and not one of his students has ever forgotten it. But as time runs along, many teachers fade from memory. He was the rare teacher who just doesn't open a door, but makes you want to run through it eagerly to see all you can.

In high school, when we came to *The Rime of the Ancient Mariner*, I asked about the dice game. The Spectre-Woman in the poem wins the throw and "whistles thrice." I asked my teacher why she whistles three times, which was obscure to me. The teacher said, "She has to — *thrice* rhymes with *dice*, up above."

"Why not *twice?*"

She said nothing about three, seven, and nine and their mystic significance, but told me this was a serious piece of literature and further frivolity about it would be unseemly. From my later experiences as a Maine author, I wonder she didn't have me write to Mr. Coleridge.

17

$\mathcal{A}$ GOOD WORD should be said for the Rotary Club. Authors start small, and are lucky if honors come to them before old-age benefits. But upon the first evidence of budding talent, every Maine author is eagerly sought by Rotary, Kiwanis, Lions, Exchange, and Optimists, and these are the nearest things we have today to the ancient patrons of the arts who spared many a genius from starving in a garret.

Anybody who has a book out, or anybody who is thinking about having a book come out, is approached by every program chairman, usually before any other program chairman. Until an author has spoken to a luncheon, he is merely "distinguished." Then he becomes "successful." An invitation to a Rotary meeting is not a Pulitzer Prize or an honorary degree, but it comes first and is recognition. Maine seems to have no other routine way to honor her authors, except for smallish things like the annual literary day of the Harpswell Garden Club. They had Zorach, the sculptor, at that one summer, and some of us old pros wondered, because Zorach had never written a book. But he told about the book he would write if he ever wrote a book, and things worked out.

The average membership of a Rotary Club is twenty-five. So at the end of a year, after (say) fifty meetings, the speakers outnumber Rotarians two to one. That's a good thing to know. Upon his first appearance to be honored by a service club, some of the mysticism will intrigue an author. Then he learns that while Rotarians sing a Rotary Club song, and the Kiwanians sing a Kiwanis song, they are both to the tune of "Down by the Old Mill Stream." One of the clubs has a stirring toast. The members lift glasses of water and say, "Not beneath you, not above you, but with you!" The fervor given this toast stirs the most sluggish heart, and gives the author a lot to think about. The bountiful repast is always a seven-rib roast of beef, delectable vegetables in abundance, and tasty gourmet desserts without end. After the meatloaf (or chicken in a patty) the author naturally expects to be called upon for his remarks, which is why he is there.

But many matters must be disposed of first. Visiting members are introduced, given applause, and allowed a few well-chosen words. Rising votes of thanks are accorded sundry committees, even to the woman who washes the dishes, and then there is a detailed report from the raffle committee. Then they give out pins for five years of perfect attendance. It is alarming to contemplate the great number of Rotarians who have never missed a meeting, but comforting to think of all the Maine authors they have honored in five years. When everything else has been disposed of, it is time to introduce "our distinguished speaker of the day." This is not done by the president, but by the chairman of the program committee, who frequently begins by saying, "We're lucky to have a speaker today at all." He explains that he tried to get this one and that one, and finally had to settle on "our distinguished guest." Invariably, the speaker needs no introduction, but ". . . without further ado, I now introduce a man who needs no introduction . . ."

Rotarians (and this includes all the others) do not hang back when the introduction has been made. They stand, clapping loudly, and this is a fine tribute and a great recognition of talent. After the speech, they do it again, and then there is always some member who comes up to say: "What is the name of your book? I'll see if the library has it."

There was a service club in Augusta that wanted to honor me, and I said I was heartsick to have to refuse, but I had several previous engagements. At that time my uncle Ralph, who was in his seventies, had become a Maine author with his *Yankee Storekeeper,* and it turned out he called me on the telephone to say he wanted to go somewhere, and would I come and drive him? So I chauffeured Uncle Ralph to speak to the very meeting I had turned down. The program chairman was barely civil, but he fawned on Uncle Ralph and the club honored him in good shape. Uncle Ralph did a good job. On the ride home he tried to give me five dollars for driving him to the meeting, but I wouldn't take it.

"It's really yours, anyway," he said. "They gave it to me to help pay for the gas."

"Is that all they gave you?"

"Well, I hadn't expected to get anything."

I said, "Welcome to the Society of Maine Authors!"

It is a tedious job to become cultural adviser to a service club. The first few visitations are instructive to both author and audience, but after a time it is small fun to stand behind a table of dirty dishes and regale shopkeepers who are fidgeting to get back to their cash registers. Noon luncheons end promptly at one o'clock, and presidents have been known to thump the gong and interrupt an author right in his best anecdote. Clubs that meet in the evening will indulge an author a mite longer, and as members linger after meeting there are occasional nuggets of inspiration derived from the fellowship. The emolument is vaporish. One wonders if the exposure sells books, but publishers seem to think it does. Uncle Sam does permit reasonable expenses, but Maine authors soon learn they cannot live by deductions alone.

But no author should make a hard-and-fast rule against being honored by Rotary. There are rewarding surprises. One of the most pleasant evenings I ever had was at a service club at Vinalhaven — Vinalhaven being an island in Penobscot Bay fifteen miles out from Rockland. Attending the evening meeting required what Maine islanders call "over a boat," which means I spent the night and returned to "the main" the next day. The supper is served by church ladies in the parish hall, but I was told to come to the Bayside Garage and Body Fixit at five-thirty, which I did. I found the membership in full tipple, since the ladies didn't brook wassail in church. The garage workbench had been cleared, and BYOBs prevailed. As the distinguished author about to be honored, I had free choice, but I could see I needed a clear head to confront this situation. Vinalhaven is the world's leading lobster port, and the membership ran to lobstermen, who are not ungifted when it comes to the choice and use of words. That evening, on Vinalhaven, I heard one of the best-told stories of my cadging career. Nobody has ever bettered the swiftness of pace, the clarity and vividness, the dramatic action, the artful denouement. The lobsterman, having gained my ear, said:

> My wife always wanted to see Disneyland, so
> we went to the main, and one day in Utah . . .

There is a phrase of eighteen words; it covers motivation, preparation, departure, a ferry ride, and two thousand miles! The lobsterman went on:

> . . . and one day in Utah I comes up behind this pickup doing maybe fifteen miles an hour, and just as I started to pass it the thing swung straight across my bow . . .

The lobsterman paused for suspense, sipped his scotch and Seven-Up, looked at me to judge the time he should wait, and went on:

> . . . and I tell you now — *there* was an accident!

Nobody disputed this. He paused again, sipped, and concluded:

> Then this joker gets out of that pickup, and I can tell you he was *some* old mad, and he yells at me, he says, "You damn fool, you — you mighta known I was goin' to turn off. I live there!"

Not too many service-club meetings will measure up to that one on Vinalhaven, but the occasional one that does compensates for the others. The Vinalhaven garage work being attended to, the members walked to the church, where the supper was superb. Afterwards, a couple of lobstermen walked me to my lodgings. We stood a few minutes looking at the moon on the harbor, the lobster boats waiting for morning. One of the lobstermen said, "Been a first-rate evening."

I said, "Finest kind."

When I got back to the main, I hesitated about charging such a good time off as a business expense. But I knew I could use that story out of Utah, so I had to.

18

THE ATTITUDE of government toward authors
is not that of a kindred spirit, and anybody thinking of going into the business should give it thought.
There is no law that I know of, local, state, and federal,
that understands what an author is, realizes how he
operates, and recognizes his oddities. There is no official who administrates any law who cares. There is
nothing in our political attitudes that amounts to
patronage of the arts. Instead, it is sporty to pick on
the writer in about every way that might discourage
him.

The effect is that while authors are not at all like
other people, they must be like other people. An
author gets no salary or wages, but he has to answer

questions about salary and wages. He has no fringes or withholding, but he must fill out forms as if he did have. He works on no schedule, keeps no hours, and has no way of dividing toil and leisure, but he must keep books just the same. He is asked to show profit-and-loss statements on the same forms used for florists, carpenters, and bank presidents, although he accumulates no tangible business property, has no stock in trade, and hasn't the faintest idea just where and when any increment accrued. He operates on a time lag, which is perfectly reasonable to a writer, but incomprehensible to all others — so the ferry ticket to Vinalhaven becomes a proper business expense twenty-five years later when the story gets printed. Because everybody else does, an author must retire at sixty-five, and it does no good to bring *De Senectute* into the Social Security office and read a bit of it to the girl. Royalty earned from July to December is paid the following April, and this simple, and universal, publishing custom causes the IRS infinite confusion.

Time and again people ask, "How long does it take you to write a book?"

Another nauseating compliment is: "You write so easily!"

A book is written from the total experience of the author, so that a first drop from a mother's pap is a business expense. If a man is eighty-five years old, that's how long it took him to write a book. And if he appears to "write easily," it is because he sweats long hours with as much labor, and a good deal more mental work, than goes into making a bridge. Blaise Pascal apologized because his letter was so long; he didn't have time, he said, to make it shorter.

The tax people had a paragraph hidden deep in the type that said literary earnings may be prorated over thirty-six months, provided that much time, or more, was spent in producing the work. Since I put about ten years into the writing of *Farmer Takes a Wife*, I was pleased to learn about this, and quickly figured out that thirty-six months to the tax people converted roughly to three years in my language, so I took my tabulations and went to the income-tax office in Augusta. Clinton Clauson was regional collector at that time, and I asked him to show me how I should make the computations. He said it would be far too complicated for his department to figure the thing out, and he wouldn't let me do it. Told me my only recourse would be to go to court. He shuffled my papers around, and said, "It does seem to me like an absurd way to have income." Uncle Sam took several thousand dollars from me that he had no right to whatever. Uncle Sam wasn't interested and didn't care.

A few years later this Clinton Clauson became governor of Maine, an occasion for prayer. Indeed, after the secretary of state swore him in, the secretary of state drew a deep breath and called out, "God save the State of Maine!"

When I became sixty-five, I was asked to appear at the Social Security office to "apply for benefits," and

the first question the girl asked was, "Are you retired?"

What does an author retire from? Years ago somebody asked a neighbor of mine what I did, and the
neighbor said, "Oh, he doesn't do anything — he
writes." When my wife and I spent four happy months
in Europe, a lot of people wished they might be a
wealthy Maine author and do the same. But it took
several printings of *Europe on Saturday Night* to pay
for our holiday, and our best profit on the book was
our memory of a good time. There are no vacations for
an author; O. O. McIntyre once wrote: A writer is
working when he's just looking out the window.

This is not a beef or a bellyache. I wouldn't have it
otherwise, and the vexations caused by the general
attitude have their amusing sides. At least, they make
something to write about. But a serenity conducive to
production is helpful in any profession.

19

MY APPRENTICESHIP in journalism began before the Crash of 1929 and lasted through the New Deal of Franklin Delano Roosevelt — whose political ambitions changed our life and living so much. The country weekly paper had not begun to imitate the dailies and still had character and style. We still had editors. There was no radio and television of consequence to compete for the advertising dollar, and a second-class postal permit was a license to steal. A single copy of the *Record* was four cents — two dollars a year by mail. The pace was leisurely, and there was always time for the editor to hand copy back and say, "This needs some polishing."

Apprenticeship on a country weekly newspaper led

to an unbounded understanding that I would have acquired in no other way. I have no hesitation in claiming that I was one of the first Americans to understand the new labor unions. Maine had been getting by with the older unions, such as that of the sulfite workers, and the arrival of the CIO was news. It hit the Cabot Mill in Brunswick, and my job was to report the organizing activities. I knew just about everybody who worked in the mill on a first-name basis, so when the first meeting was called I wandered down to the hall on Mill Street.

I stood on the sidewalk talking to old friends, and at the appointed hour started to go into the building. A character I did not know because he was shipped-in talent stopped me at the door and said this meeting was strictly for workers in the Cabot Mill, and publicity was not desired. This fellow could have been cast in any Al Capone gangster documentary, and I was a little hurt that none of my Cabot Mill friends interceded. They passed by me on the other side. It is most informative to see warm friendships thus dissipate when outsiders appeal, and I came away with my own thoughts about the CIO. I asked a couple of fellows afterwards what happened and was able to produce a short news story that I thought was hardly "publicity."

I was next told that at the second meeting, this Capone character stood up on the platform, waved a copy of the previous *Record,* and shouted: "This shows what an uphill fight we have on our hands!

Even your local newspaper is against you! Why didn't the *Record* give us a good story?" And so on. It isn't much fun to deal with that kind of contrivance, but my understanding was enlarged. Understanding makes better writing.

There was another story about that time that shows how a trifling distinction can aid the writer. Just before Christmas we were having a diphtheria epidemic. Little yellow quarantine tags were all over town, and fear and anxiety ran faster than the contagion. The storekeepers were doing no Christmas business at all; people stayed home and out-of-towners shunned us. As the disease raged, swabs were taken of every school child and sent to the state laboratory at Augusta. The daily papers were giving Brunswick a black eye with every issue, and it was time for me to write my hometown report.

When the telephone rang, it was Dr. Earl Richardson at the Brunswick Hospital. "I've been thinking," he said, "that the hospital ought to do a little something for Christmas. We're having a little party this evening, and I want you to come."

I went, and it was a nice party. The off-duty nurses greeted us wearing pretty frocks, ushered us in, and later served ice cream and cake. There was a decorated tree in the corner of the reception room. All the physicians in Brunswick were there, and I noticed also that Dr. Coombs, our state director of health and welfare, had come down from Augusta. And a number of businessmen. Dr. Richardson was shaking hands and explaining that this was just a little gesture to get good folks together. He had a special guest, he said, who had promised to "entertain."

The special guest turned out to be a Dr. Plaice, who was chief of the contagion ward at the Boston City Hospital. When he rose to "entertain" us, he began by saying, "Of course, there isn't a true case of diphtheria in the whole town of Brunswick."

Dr. Plaice continued as if lecturing to first-year nurses. He explained that diphtheria can be present without infection, and that the germs can be found in people who aren't sick at all. He turned to Dr. Coombs and said, "Have you been making virulency tests?"

Dr. Coombs was an old-school man, affecting a beard, and he was close to retirement. He wasn't happy at this prying into the official affairs of his laboratory, so he sputtered a bit before saying, "No." Then he added, "This epidemic struck so fast that we have neither the equipment nor the staff to pursue virulency."

Dr. Plaice calmly went on: "I appreciate how that is, but I've noticed that diphtheria epidemics subside almost immediately if virulency tests are specified."

Ours in Brunswick subsided the next day, and I wrote a short paragraph about the lovely Christmas party at the Brunswick Hospital. Dr. Richardson was an able surgeon, but he was also a wise man, and as long as I covered Brunswick news he was careful to keep me rightly informed about stories that concerned him, his hospital, and public health. He wanted me to understand. I think the CIO never did.

Not too many people dealing with reporters are that wise. There was a lawyer who gave me considerable trouble, but he likewise furthered my understanding. There was a grocery store that went bankrupt, and the sheriff put a big padlock on the front door. But the storekeeper was selling goods out the back door, and I went around and bought a broom for ten cents — accompanied by a reliable witness to the transaction. Then I went to see this lawyer, who was handling the bankruptcy, and he gave me the stupid "no comment" routine. I reasoned that I had given him a chance, and when the *Record* appeared he howled a good deal. He shouted about the right to privacy of his abused client, and I said, "If you give me ten cents, you can have the broom back." A lawyer for one of the creditors, however, went out of his way to come into the office and thank me, and gave me a cigar. The understanding that accrued has pleased me.

Another time there was a shoe factory owner who thought to settle unrest among his workers by posting a notice asking everybody to check with the paymaster and see that his record was correct. A wage increase was being contemplated, the notice said, and attention should be immediate. I saw the notice, and so did all the workers — who promptly went to the paymaster. But the owner had no intention of increasing wages, and I suspected that. On the other hand, higher shoe shop pay is news, so I had a squib about the notice in the next issue. We were at once visited by a lawyer who said: "You have placed my client in a bad business position! There was never any such notice!"

Thus is understanding inculcated. Our editor was fussed up, and to ward off a lawsuit he agreed to run a retraction and write an apology. When he asked me to write the retraction, I refused. "Retract what?" I asked. "The notice was up, everybody saw it, and this scheming character should apologize to us!

"Tell you what I'll do," I said. "You tell this lawyer if he'll forget the whole thing, I'll give him back the notice I swiped off the bulletin board." It shows what understanding can lead to.

Our office girl took some notes over the telephone one day and left them on my desk — it happened all the time. An elderly couple had had an anniversary, and the neighborhood had joined in a party for the occasion. The notes were sketchy and brief, but they told me all I needed to know. The couple had received many gifts, and the guests had played cards and enjoyed refreshments. After the paper was out, I found I had misinterpreted the notes — the guests had *not* played cards because these folks were of a religious group that is opposed to cards. They had *received* greeting cards. I imagine the *Record* was truly wide open to libel on that one. I got a bouquet and a box of chocolates and called on the elderly couple, and disaster was averted. One must always understand.

I turned in a story one day about a prominent

Brunswick man who had committed suicide. He put a
.45-caliber revolver in his mouth and pulled the
trigger. Our editor of the moment was overfriendly
with that family, and he allowed this friendship to
temper his editorial judgment. He doctored the suicide story so it appeared as a simple obituary saying
the man had "died suddenly." It was a long time before the *Record* got over that one. I'd be walking
along the street and somebody would call at me:
"Died suddenly! Haw, haw, haw!" "He sure did!" was
the greeting I got from many.

I labored for about ten years with the *Record*, and
it was excellent training. When the circulation of the
Record was audited at 4500 paid copies weekly — an
excellent figure for that community — Frank Nichols,
the owner, shook my hand and said, "You've done us a
fine job — I think this calls for a drink!"

No, he did not haul a quart of scotch from a desk
drawer. He walked me across the street to Wilson's
Drug Store, and we each had a strawberry ice-cream
soda. You've got to understand things like that, too.

20

WHEN A Maine "pa'tridge" flies up from underfoot, even if you half expect him, the explosion of his wings will startle. It is, all the same, a joyful experience to be scairt that way by a ruffed grouse, and to see him scale off through the trees. Likewise, one of the finest things to happen to an author, or an editor, is to have a story, a book, an essay take off like a bat from the hot place and astonish everybody. Even the most experienced editors and writers are never sure if this will happen. It can be contrived sometimes, but more often it is a surprise.

There is a story about one editor who was short of copy for his weekly paper, so in desperation at the last minute he set the telephone directory in type. "Following," he wrote, "are the names listed in the local telephone directory." It sounds absurd until you analyze it; everybody with a telephone looked to see if he was there, and getting people to look is the editor's first function. But this chap was not only an editor, he was a good editor, and he left out about two dozen names on purpose.

Then came about two dozen letters from people who wanted "to set the record straight," and he was able to get extra mileage another week. Letters to the editor are the comebackers that prove a pa'tridge has taken off.

My best pa'tridge was the three-tined fork. My wife lost her three-tined kitchen fork and was lost without it. She couldn't turn bacon, scramble eggs, and punch potatoes to see if they were done. I wrote a lament for the three-tined fork, and the fun began. I would never have predicted such success with that topic. Letters came in bundles, and within a few weeks we received over four hundred three-tined kitchen forks from sympathetic ladies all over the world. Some who wrote said, "If you find one, I'd like one, too," so we became fork exchangers. This set up a pen-pal cycle, and before we got through our postage bill came to a good deal more than I got for writing the piece.

The mustache cup did well. When the hippies brought whiskers back, I assumed the crockery shops would rally and begin offering old-fashioned mustache cups. This proved to be not so; the potters were asleep at their wheels. I did the obvious essay, urging hippies to demand their rights. The reader response to mustache cups was incredible; I heard from everybody during the next few weeks, including a shop in London ready to supply them in left-handed models.

The trout in the well was good. We had a small item that a man had put a trout in his well. In Maine, this needs no explanation. Dug wells catch grasshoppers and other insects, even if covered, and a brook trout eats them. The trout does the water no harm, and many a well without a trout has been known to "go flat" — the water becomes off-taste. So this man put a trout in his well, and we had an item. Some readers who didn't know about trout in wells thought the farmer was making a kind of pound, so he could go out and get trout for breakfast when he wished, and the mail began to come in. When we printed letters that doubted the trout, the letters from people who knew all about them followed. The thing was a beautiful comebacker for several weeks, and then it got out of hand.

Well, a game warden came in to tell us he had just extricated a moose from an abandoned well in the woods up back, and the next week a veterinarian came in to tell us he had treated a cow for immersion — she fell in a well. A sequence like this makes it easy to get out a paper. And the next week came Leon Bard's midnight call on Dr. Plummer.

Somebody was teaming a load of logs, and a horse broke through planks and went into a well. They got him out with a gantry and he seemed all right except he was chilled. They covered him and put lighted lanterns under the blankets, but he shook a lot. They telephoned to a veterinarian at a distance, and he suggested they give the horse two ounces of whiskey every hour until he seemed all right.

So Leon Bard set out in the middle of the night to find some whiskey in a temperance town in a state that had been legally dry since the time of Neal Dow. As a last resort, he tolled the doorbell of A. W. Plummer, M.D., who came out in his dressing gown. "Well, hello, Leon," said Dr. Plummer.

Leon said, "Doc, I need some whiskey."

Doc said, "So do I, come on in."

The rest of the story was that the horse didn't like the whiskey and fought it all the way. But at the end of an hour when they gave him two more ounces, he wasn't quite so set against taking it. At the end of another hour, the horse reached up for the bottle.

They made a drunkard out of that horse.

All because some farmer put a trout in his well.

There was a lawyer in Brunswick named G. Allen Howe, and I found him a constant source for items and stories. It got so he would look for things I could use. When he and his wife went to a shore-dinner restaurant, he liked the clam chowder so well he asked the chef for the recipe.

"Put this in the paper," he said. "It's the best clam chowder I ever stuck a tooth in, and I think the women will like to have it."

I printed it the way he gave it to me. The first line was:

Take forty quarts whole milk . . .

Just about every housewife in town wrote in about that, and we had letters to the editor enough for a while.

21

ONE OF MY pleasantest writing chores was to work with the editors of *Down East* magazine on a book they finally called *Maine Lingo.* It was an opportunity to sift, collate, and explain a great many things that constantly give a Maine author concern. It's not unlike Germany, where a scholarly society of translators recently said all books in that language should be printed in two editions, because Bavarians do not understand North German. Any Maine author with experience will think perhaps six editions will serve the United States.

An example from the German translators was illustrative. One of our generals when we were nursing the war in Vietnam said a certain military maneuver "didn't come within a thousand miles of success." A Munich newspaper translated this to say: "The action occurred at a distance of 1600 kilometers." Some things don't translate, and the Maine vernacular can be an exercise in frustration. I once referred to a person as a "jillpoke," and I got letters from all across the country telling me there is no such word. I looked in the dictionary, and these people were right. There is no such word.

When lumbering began and drives of long logs came down the Maine rivers to mill, now and then a persnickety log would turn crosswise of the stream and cause a jam — a logjam. This brought great work and much danger to the river drivers, who came to call this particular log the jillpoke. So in Maine anybody who does booby things and causes trouble is a damn jillpoke. It's a Maine word.

The philologist often falters. Here in Maine our fishermen build a stand on the prow of their boats from which they launch harpoons at horsefish. These stands are called *pulpits*. A lexicographer will naturally suppose they are called pulpits because they are up front, like a pulpit in church; the fisherman is like a minister. The exact opposite is true: the pulpit in church is so called because it is up front like the stand on a boat. The minister is like a harpoonist. When anybody in Maine "takes the pulpit," he's the one's goin' to heave the lily iron.

I got into some indelicacies with *fly-time*. I told a Flats Jackson story about a camp cook who spoiled his pot hellion with too much salt. Flats explained this by saying, "It was all fly-time with him!" When the letters came asking what *fly-time* might mean, it was difficult to find a genteel explanation. The full Maine expression is "Tight as a bull's backside in fly-time." Except that we do not use the euphemism *backside*. Reference is to the persistence of the native Maine blackfly and the difficulty a bull has in protecting that part of his anatomy. All he can do is sort of draw things together. And tightness is a form of inebriation. The camp cook, making the stew, was over the bay. He was tighter'n a fiddler's bitch. Tighter'n a constipated hoot owl. Hotter'n a skunk. He was drunk. It was all fly-time with him.

My use of *haul*, over the years, has used up more than a few blue pencils in editorial offices and has brought me hundreds of letters. *Haul* supplants all other words in Maine for pulling, lifting, dragging, moving, and related actions. What other people would call "lumbering roads," we called "log-hauls." Water is hauled from a well in a pail, then hauled to the house by hand. A man hauls on his boots. One hauls his wife to town so she can do the shopping. Boats are hauled for repairs, sails are hauled, and if you back down from a position you haul in your sails. Lobstermen haul their traps, and their daily catch is their haul. All this is explained in *Maine Lingo*, but all Maine authors have been using it naturally since the beginnings.

When I wrote, years ago, that Mother hauled the hot biscuits from the oven, I got my first letter about *haul:* "What did she haul them with, a yoke of oxen?" Sometimes an editor will change *haul* to *draw,* and this is as un-Maine as a desert cactus. We draw "pitchers," and we draw pensions, and winter drawers on, but we haul pulpwood and children to school and we haul in our ears instead of pulling them in. "Haul off your pants," says the doctor; or if he's giving a shot he says, "Haul up your sleeve."

Every single time, I believe, that I have told how some haymaker was "building load," out-of-state editors changed it to "building a load." "Tending store" invariably comes out in print as "minding the store." And most of all, editors love to change *some* to *somewhat.* When it is some hot in Maine, that does not mean it is somewhat hot. It means an old scorcheroo. When it gets hotter than just plain "some hot," it gets "some old hot." "By gawd, that pie was some old good!" said my lobsterman Harold after "taking" supper with us, and my wife beamed. She likes compliments. My uncle Ralph used to tell about the old fellow in Harmony who stood up a ladder and inadvertently punched the glass out of an upstairs window. He was some old mad, now I tell you. *Somewhat* doesn't fit.

So the Maine author has the constant problem of writing the Maine vernacular for many people who can't come within 1600 kilometers of its beauty. And biggest problem of all are the poetic images editors still find objectionable, even though pornography is rampant. Even the *Down East* editors wouldn't let me put into *Maine Lingo* the excessively nice lady who thinks she "defecates" ice cream, even though one can hear her referred to frequently in the vicinity of the editorial offices. I have never, until now, got into print the dog who is so lucky he has — how shall I say it now? — two members. A dog with twice the usual equipment is considered some old lucky along the Maine coast. And the flatus! The one caught in a gale of wind, and the one running around in a mitten. Blue-penciled, all, and yet how long ago was it that Squire Western, himself, used a fart in *Tom Jones* as literary punctuation?

22

M ILLIONS HAVE BOUGHT boots and fly dope
and "outdoor specialties" from L. L. Bean, but
few realize this Freeport mail-order genius also wrote
books and was the most successful of all Maine authors. He was just another of these iodine-laden Maine
characters who took a deep breath one morning and
started to write. He made more money with his *Hunting, Fishing and Camping* than all the rest of us put
together. No university ever gave the slightest thought
to awarding him a Litt.D., and all professional publishers who looked at Mr. Bean's literary effort were
nauseated — but the book went on and on through
printing after printing, blithely wafting a faint cul-

tural scent through the profusion of leather goods, fishing tackle, and sportswear sent postage-paid all over the world.

Mr. Bean began his mail-order career in 1911 — he was born in 1872. The famous "Maine Hunting Shoe" with which he started had been joined by hundreds of other items, and all had made him a millionist by 1940, when he first thought of writing a book. I was a party to his literary career from the first, and have always felt honored that a photograph I made of Mr. Bean was the frontispiece in his unweighty tome. In 1935 he came home from New Brunswick with a great bull moose and I snapped the picture with "Mr. Bean is on the right." Over the years since, as that picture has appeared in books, catalogs, circulars, and advertising, it has become one of the most frequently published photographs. Because Mr. Bean and I were close friends, I made him a present of the negative long ago, whereas I might have held out for residuals and become wealthy along with him.

Mr. Bean was a chummy man, and as he built his business the whole town of Freeport was interested and played a part. For example: One day I walked into his office and he had maybe a hundred axes of various makes and patterns leaning against the walls. Each had a shipping tag attached. Mr. Bean had decided his catalog needed an ax that was light enough to carry on a trail, but heavy enough for useful chopping. He wanted, also, a distinctive pattern. So every firm that made axes was invited to submit samples, and here they all were lined up in L.L.'s office. "Pick out the one you like," he said.

I hefted them, tested the hang, and said, "This one."

"Good," he said, and he made a note on the shipping tag. After everybody in Freeport had done the same and he had a popularity score, he put Freeport's favorite ax in his catalog and it is still there.

He approached his literary career in the same way. I came in that morning in 1940 and he said, "I've got a little idea I think you can help me with." In 1940 I had not had a book published, but *New England Town Meeting* was about to appear. As newspaper reporter I had, however, climbed the two flights of stairs to Mr. Bean's office at least once a week for a long time. His door was always open. "Come in!" he'd boom. "Got somebody here wants to meet you!" Once it was Jack Dempsey. Another time it was Eleanor Roosevelt. On that day, he was alone, and he said he was thinking of writing a book. A handbook on outdoor fun — how to set up a tent, how to dress out a deer, Mr. Bean's own personal opinions about the fields, streams, and forests. Having just had dealings with a trade publisher over *Town Meeting*, I offered my thoughts in that direction, but I soon realized Mr. Bean was not all that interested. No Maine author, or any other author, went about his book as did Mr. Bean.

As we say in Maine, he had his world by the tail on a downhill cant. His own printing plant in his own factory could print the thing — just yank out the form on winter footgear and stick in the book. Mr. Bean saw no reason to submit his manuscript to a publisher and await a decision. His catalog experts could tell him if the book would sell more copies out of page sixteen than it would out of page twenty-four, just as they could with bedrolls and ski boots. I was particularly amused about his idea of size.

He wanted to keep the price of the book at one dollar — and since each copy cost him thirty-two cents this seemed fine to me. I suppose it sounds like the best royalty in the history of publishing, but it is not — because on succeeding printings he got his figures down to twenty-three cents. The price of a dollar was predicated on a customer's willingness to add that to his order. After sending for canoe shoes, underwear, a set of flannel shirts, ski boots, and a sleeping bag, a customer would think little of one more dollar and would buy a book. So the book must be small enough so it would tuck into the bundle and not increase the postage. It also had to be small enough so that single copies could be mailed at the minimum rate. The book went through Mr. Bean's factory like sweat shirts and bucktail flies. It carried his usual guarantee of money back if not satisfied, and it was always "postpaid."

His mail-order necessity for keeping the book under a hundred pages led to his first sentence in the introduction: "It is not my purpose to bore my readers, but to bring reliable information in the fewest possible words." He pointed out that the whole book could be read in less than eighty minutes. The elapsed time, however, included some repetition, since five of his chapters were duplicated. This was so readers could cut them out to be carried on the trail in a pocket without spoiling the book.

Mr. Bean and his catalog experts erred in estimating spring sales for the first edition. Five thousand copies were not enough, and a second printing of ten thousand kept the presses running nights. The thing went through fifteen printings before Mr. Bean revised it, and at that time I wrote a "review" of his literary career for *The New York Times Book Review*. Any author likes to be reviewed favorably by the *Times*, and L.L. was delighted. But after an appropriate interval he told me the exposure in the *Times* had not produced the sales he had expected. His office girls had been "keying" the review in the *Times* the same way they keyed all L. L. Bean advertising. The book then went through another dozen or so printings before sales tapered off and the catalog space was given over to other things.

I have the first bound copy of *Hunting, Fishing and Camping* by L. L. Bean — Maine author. He picked it off the pile in the printshop and wrote on the flyleaf:

> To John Gould
> from one
> *author??*
> to another
> — *L. L. Bean*

It has a neoprene binding so if it gets wet in a canoe it won't hurt it too much.

23

WHAT O. O. McIntyre really wrote was: "A woman can live all her life with a writer and not learn he is working when he's just looking out the window." Must have been that old "Odd" had an interrupting wife, and when I read that in his column I felt sorry for him. My wife quickly learned her role in my career. We had been married just a short time when I was sitting in the kitchen talking to Will Andrews. Will was a Maine character, a fine yarner about the old days in the woods, and after he had a small shock he had little to do but sit around and yarn. (In Maine, you have a "shock," not a "stroke.") He'd come shuffling up the road with two canes, his dog at his heels, and settle into our kitchen rocker. There we were one day, and Will was telling me about a big logjam on the West Branch back when he was young.

The telephone rang, and I heard my wife say, "I'm sorry, he can't come to the phone now — he's working on a story."

When isn't he?

I'd take a lunch, grind the farm tractor up into the woodlot, and spend the day manufacturing firewood. Toward evening I'd bring a load down, stack it by the woodshed, and come into the house. To some wives, I suppose this would mean a busy day — was it cold? how much did I cut? was the lunch all right? did the tractor get hung up on a stump? did the G.D. chainsaw run? But not my understanding wife. Her one question was always: "Did you get anything?"

One evening I said, "Saw one rabbit eight times."

Which I did. I'd been working about an hour when this rabbit bounded into my clearing, just hitting the high spots, and he stopped to chew on the tops I'd dropped. Off in the distance I could hear a hound bugling, and as the hound was on the scent of this rabbit, the dog came closer. The rabbit chewed awhile, standing up now and then to listen to the dog, and just as the dog was about to come into the clearing the rabbit took off at top speed and was gone. Then the dog came into sight, sniffed where the rabbit had paused to eat, and kept on going. As the rabbit made his circle, he'd come back to my clearing, eat some more, and then take off as the dog approached. Neither animal paid the slightest heed to me. The rabbit was completely at ease while eating at my tops, seemingly enjoying the good run he was giving the dog. Eight times they went by that day.

We had supper, and in the lamplight session she said, "I keep thinking about that rabbit."

"What about him?"

"I keep wondering about how you'll use him."

Not a word about the wood I cut, the lunch, the stumps, the chainsaw.

Interruptions at the desk, while the manuscript is being written, are not critical. I can leave off in mid-sentence and return. Before I begin writing I have my yarn in mind, my thoughts in some order, and the task is pretty well finished. One day while I was finishing a book she came from upstairs and said, "I feel like going for a ride." We went for a ride. We passed the first night in Fredericton, New Brunswick, and went on to tour the Gaspé. In two weeks we came home and I finished the book. She knew a ride would not be an interruption at that time and felt a few days away would be refreshing. On such rides, she holds a notebook and jots down random ideas for future reference. "That's good for a piece!" she'll say. She helps me look out the window.

One time she came from the store with a new towel rack for the bathroom. "Put it up when you're not looking out the window," she said. "I want it to go right there."

"It can't go there."

"Why not?"

"The studs come wrong. I can put it here, or I can put it here. But not there."

"Can't you use longer screws?"

"Not in Sheetrock. It just won't go there."

I explained about a man's world that sets studs sixteen inches on center, and she said, "I'll bet you get a piece out of that!" I did.

In the serenity of my own household, where looking out the window is recognized as a writer's honest labor, I've always wondered about Mrs. McIntyre.

24

BEING TAGGED as a "humorist" early in my career has been a burden ever since. 'Twas Molière who said making gentlemen laugh is a strange business. A German observed that one may write amusingly and still be serious. Bill Nye had a piece about how to tell the humorist at a party — he's the sad little man off by himself looking ill. The time I was lumped with the great comics was a dreary experience.

One of these national magazines that circulates as supplement to Sunday newspapers was doing a series about the ten favorite jokes. I'd seen a couple of the pieces. One was about Jack Benny, who told his ten favorite jokes. They had Henny Youngman, and others. One day the man telephoned me from New York and said he was flying to Maine to take my picture and hear my ten favorite jokes.

Writing anything, humor included, involves roughly the same industrial methods as grinding sausage. From certain ingredients, in a certain way, you turn out a product. It is a business, and it has tricks that must be mastered. I was talking one time with "Doc" Rockwell, the veteran vaudeville comedian. We were discussing the dog-eared old gags of the Keith-Orpheum circuits that made audiences laugh year in and year out. I brought up this one:

COMIC: Our dog doesn't eat meat.
STRAIGHT MAN: You're dog doesn't eat meat?
COMIC: No, our dog doesn't eat meat.
STRAIGHT MAN: Why doesn't your dog eat meat?
COMIC: We don't give him any.

Doc shook his head. "You're right, and you're wrong," he said. "*Meat* isn't a funny word. It has to be *beefsteak*. Our dog doesn't eat beefsteak. I don't know why, but I know beefsteak will get a better laugh than meat."

So anything meant to be funny must be seriously considered in the funny-mill. This fellow who came up from New York was a nice-enough chap, and he knew his own trade all right. But as we talked, I could see that we were miles apart in our ideas. He seemed to think I should turn on a spigot and gush hilarity. I tried to tell him my Maine yarns and stories were hardly in the Bob Hope range, and he continued to talk about "gags."

I told him one of my favorite Maine stories is about the river driver who had spent a winter in the lumber camp and was now down in Bangor ready and willing for a big feed of something besides baked beans and salt horse. He went into the dining room at the Bangor House and ordered the lobster bisque, the steamed clams, the fried clams, two boiled lobsters. Then he had a steak and eggs, with fried potatoes and boiled onions, with a side order of cold cuts. Then he asked what kind of pie they had.

The waitress said, "Apple, pineapple, strawberry-rhubarb, apricot, coconut-cream, cherry, lemon, and custard."

"Good!" he says. "Bring me a piece each of apple, pineapple, strawberry-rhubarb, apricot, coconut-cream, cherry, and lemon."

The waitress said, "What's the matter with our custard pie?"

The man from the magazine looked at me for some time. As Mark Twain said, "That joke was lost on the foreigner." The man from the magazine said, "You've got to have something better than that."

I said I had a couple of woodchuck stories.

He said, "Let's hear them."

I told him about the farmer whose dog put a woodchuck in the wall, and as the woodchuck was safe down under the rocks the farmer came to lift them away and let the dog get at the 'chuck. The woodchuck was chittering away, driving the dog to a frenzy, and as the farmer lifted, the dog kept jumping back and forth over the stone wall. When the farmer finally uncovered the 'chuck, the dog was on the far side.

So the farmer hit the woodchuck with a club. "But," I told the man from the magazine, "when the club came down, the dog had darted back, and he was under the club when it came down."

The man looked at me again. "This is funny?"

"Yes, you see — to this day the dog thinks the woodchuck killed him."

"Try again."

"Well, the other woodchuck story is about the two farm boys who played woodchuck. When you play woodchuck, one boy sticks his head out of a hole in the foundation of the barn, and the other one hits him with a bat. So one boy stuck his head out, and his brother hit him with a club. Then the boy who was the woodchuck said, ' 'Twarn't no fair — no fair! You didn't give me time to chitter!' "

"I suppose you have some other favorites?"

"Well, there's the fellow with liver complaint who found a mineral spring up in Hebron that cured him. He lived there twenty years, drinking this water in perfect health."

"So?"

"Well, when this man came to die, the coroner had to take his liver out and kill it with a club."

In explaining that Maine stories like to ramble along and rarely have the snapper of a good stage gag, I told this man he should consider the story about the girl who sat on a porcupine.

"How does it go?"

"Well, it goes any number of ways. It winds around, and relates all the details of the girl's anguish, the concern of everybody present, the difficulty of extricating the quills, and the great relief that leads to the punch line."

"Which is?"

"The punch line is: 'And that's how the leather boat-cushion came to be invented.'"

"I see."

Then I told him about Horace Jordan and his Jersey heifer. Horace came to see my grandfather one time with this heifer tied to the tailgate of his wagon, and he wanted "service." For use of a bull, Grandfather charged fifty cents, and he had a number of bulls. But at the moment they were all up in the pasture. So Horace drove his wagon up the lane to the pasture, where the bulls stood in a circle ready for business, and Horace looked them all over and said, "I'll take that one."

About that time things got out of hand, and before Horace could larrup his old horse out of the pasture each bull had consoled the heifer several times.

Grandfather used to say, "Horace Jordan died still owing me thirty-eight dollars."

The fellow from the magazine went back to New York.

A few weeks later I was in his magazine with my ten favorite jokes — ten good New York gags I'd never heard before.

25

IN RENDERING due literary thanks to my cousin Ralph, I must be careful in separating his several sides, for if I should merely recite some of the stories about him, folks might suppose him some kind of nut. He is not. Starting with a Model T Ford and borrowed money, he artfully brought prosperity to himself and others about him and retired in November of 1970 from his own substantial business. Almost every time we visit he reveals a new interest I hadn't heard about, and his many sides range from blowing a cornet to building clocks, from sailing boats to gilding weather-cocks.

Ralph and I had a common great-grandfather, which is to say he came down on one side and I on the other. Ralph, for all his business acumen, his many charities, his public services, his hobbies, and his soft-spoken — often inaudible — voice, has been an indefatigable perpetrator of what those who don't understand have always called practical jokes. His wife Louise — whom he called Madame Defarge — once said: "I'm thankful Ralph's humor was never malicious. I hate to think what he might have done in malice or anger."

I, and a good number of my readers, will always be in his debt for his woodchuck story. One of Ralph's neighbors took pride in a beautiful flower garden, and one spring he was distraught that a woodchuck had moved in and was eating his tender seedlings. He went to a hardware store and bought one of these "humane" traps. Made of wire, it doesn't hurt the animal, or so I understand. He baited it, and the next morning found his woodchuck inside. Pleased to be so easily rid of the pest, he drove in his automobile from Cape Elizabeth, through South Portland and Portland, and up to the Blackstrap section of Falmouth where he released the animal.

Wondering if there might be a second woodchuck, he baited the trap again, and the next morning he did, indeed, have a second woodchuck. The second, he thought, looked suspiciously like the first, and the thought crossed his mind that woodchucks, like pigeons, might have a homing instinct and he had really caught the same animal twice. Improbable as this might be, he nevertheless acted upon the thought, and he drove far beyond Falmouth, almost up to Bridgton, before he let the animal loose. When he got home he set the trap again.

The next morning he had a third woodchuck — or was it the same one a third time? He hadn't seen one bit of difference. So he went into his garage and got the spray can of purple paint with which he colored identification sticks for his posies, and through the wire of the trap he painted his woodchuck purple. Now he would know if the thing kept coming back. He drove away over to Meredith, New Hampshire, and released the purple pest.

My cousin Ralph, who knew all about this woodchuck from the beginning, now went to a pet shop he knew about in Scarborough, and he said to the lady, "Do you have any woodchucks?"

Yes, she did. She had three. Ralph picked the one that most closely matched the three villains in the flower bed, and she said it would cost twelve dollars. Ralph said he would take it if she would spray it purple with this can of paint. There was a small contretemps — she had to be assured the paint was positively nontoxic, and then her curiosity wanted to know why? Ralph looked all about with an FBI caution, making sure nobody could hear, and he said, "It's a government project." She sprayed the woodchuck.

Before Ralph left, she said, "If you are just on a project, and aren't going to harm the little fellow, I'll buy him back afterwards for six dollars."

That night Ralph sneaked the little fellow into the humane trap. The next morning the flower man telephoned the Portland papers that he had a most remarkable story to tell about homing woodchucks. "All the way from Meredith, New Hampshire!" he said. He even got a little time on the radio.

Later, after some of the excitement had abated, Ralph succeeded in getting his woodchuck back, and the lady did give him six dollars. "I take it the project was a success?" she asked.

"Oh, yes," said Ralph.

We watched the papers after that, hoping some farmer over around Meredith would report a purple woodchuck . . .

Once in a great while somebody gets around to setting Ralph up. When the Cape Elizabeth fire department went after a new ambulance, the boys purposely stayed away from Ralph when they were soliciting contributions. Ralph upbraided them. "You know I like to help out on things like that — why didn't you come to me?"

No, they said, he'd done enough. Time and again they'd had his contributions for this and that, and they thought they'd let him sit this one out. "Well," said Ralph, "I'd still like to help."

"No, everything's paid for. Everything except the lettering."

"Well, there — good! Let me pay for the lettering. Have it done and send me the bill."

They brought the ambulance around to Ralph's house a few evenings later to let him see the lettering. On each side of the sleek coach it said:

Cape Elizabeth Volunteer Fire Department Community Ambulance

Then they gave him the bill. With the gold leaf, the letters cost several hundred dollars, and they told him if he was going to have a heart attack they were ready for a first run . . .

When one crosses from Portland to South Portland on "the million-dollar bridge" (its price back in the 'teens) there is a one-way traffic situation called Waterman Drive. At one place there is a small monument in the form of a lighthouse that marks a historical spot. Atop the lighthouse is a clock with a thirty-inch diameter, and nearly everybody checks the time as he drives by. One day people were amused to see three-inch letters across the front of this clock:

TIMEX

To the motorists passing, that's all it amounted to, but Ralph put up the letters with forethought.

He had also arranged for a suit of coveralls from a uniform supply house, lettered across the back:

General Time Corp.
Scranton, Pennsylvania

And he made a picture of a man in these coveralls, back to, up on a ladder as if adjusting the clock. He then caused a letter to be written to the General Time Corporation, with this picture enclosed, saying a client was interested in these thirty-inch clocks, and would they forward prices and delivery terms on one gross.

It wasn't really worth it, but it helps explain my precious cousin Ralph. The Timex people, hardly daring to deny a clock with their name on it, wrote, "We no longer make clocks — only watches." Timex never made clocks.

There are others. Ralph goes on and on, and I count him among my assets. As fellow travelers in our disrespect for computers and what they've done to us, we almost went into the cigar business. Ralph likes to relax after supper with a cigar, and once he noticed the label on a box said, "These cigars contain tobacco and tobacco substitutes." The next morning he wrote a letter to the president of the cigar company to ask what "tobacco substitutes" might be.

The letter he received in reply was one of these robot-typed things right out of the computerized office of the consumer-relations manager, and while it weasel-worded somewhat, it did answer the question. The Food & Drug people insist on certain terminology, but tobacco substitutes are, indeed, tobacco. "To thank you for your interest in our products," the letter concluded, "we are sending you a complimentary box of cigars which we hope you enjoy."

Most of us would let the matter ride there, but Ralph is not the most of us, and that also is a trifling distinction. He mulled this over, somewhat angered at a robot letter, and in two weeks he wrote to the president of the cigar company again and asked him what tobacco substitutes might be. He got the same letter again, and another box of cigars.

I said, "How long has this been going on?"

"Since a year ago last April."

And thanks to computers and robots, he still has free cigars in ample supply.

Ralph read one of my disguised pieces about himself, and wrote, "I recognize the tune, but you have changed the names to protect the guilty."

26

GRANDFATHER Thomas, who didn't make much of a father to my father, became a good grandfather to me, and all my memories of him are happy. From the time I was ten I spent considerable time with him on the old farm that later became mine. Since the Big Divorce he had lived alone there in the house his father had built, on the land his father had cleared. I never arrived but he would say, "I'm so glad you came — it gets lonely here." He philosophized so many things into my understanding that I scarce know where to begin. Perhaps with the Bible.

One winter evening he had the cat on his knee, his feet on the hearth of the range, and he asked me to read the Bible to him. To me, the Bible was the rule and guide of our faith that pious people carried to church. I had endured the Congregational Sunday-school sessions that held it to be the Word of God. I approached reading the Bible from that opinion. When Gramp dozed, his head angling, I was in the middle of some Old Testament begats — genealogical recitations of the antediluvian generations. I skipped a page.

Gramp roused, tensing the tomcat, and he said, "You skipped."

This I admitted.

"You shouldn't. Those people lived, and went their way, and the only thing we know about them is what you skipped. We owe them respect. Go back."

The day Thomas was eighteen he enlisted in Company I of the Sixteenth Maine Regiment of Volunteers. A hundred boys from his area went off in Company I to fight Abraham Lincoln's war, and afterwards five of them came home. The Sixteenth was reduced on the first day of Gettysburg to thirty-seven officers and men; Gramp fired his musket eighteen times that day. Before Gettysburg, the Sixteenth Maine was a part of the "Blanket Brigade."

By the usual idiocy of the War Department, five regiments got lost. Two from Massachusetts, two from Pennsylvania, and the Sixteenth from Maine. These had bivouacked just north of Washington, and there they stayed, forgotten. No wagons came with supplies, no orders came to move. Uniforms rotted off the soldiers, and they had to forage to survive. Gramp, off a farm, knew how to slaughter animals they liberated, and he could cook in a pail. He became something of a legend among the men as they waited out the time. When at last these five regiments were remembered, a general came to look them over, and after his inspection he wrote, "The Sixteenth Maine are the poorest soldiers but the best scavengers in the Union Army."

When the men moved forward at last, they were in pitiful condition. Still largely unsupplied, they marched toward the front, and were made to parade through Washington. In pure modesty, they wrapped what was left of the blankets about them, and thus became the Blanket Brigade. I heard about all this in the evenings as Grandfather and I sat by the stove.

His father died while he was at war. A younger brother soon "went out west," to homestead in North Dakota, and Grandfather had the old farm. He frequently said, "It's fun to make things grow," and I shared in this fun, with crops, animals, and my own growing-up. I came one late May so I could take him to the Decoration Day exercises, and found him in the long field setting his tomato plants. He grew at least an acre of tomatoes every season and always brought ripe fruits to market long before anybody else. I came along with a hoe and helped him finish the piece, but when I stood my first plant up and brought dirt about its roots, he said, "No, not like that. Lay it down."

"Everybody stands tomato plants up," he said. "But the right way is to bury everything except the very top. Roots form right away along the whole stem, and you gain about two weeks." It's fun to make things grow.

When we had finished the piece, he said, "All right, pick out the plant you think will have the first ripe tomato!" I selected a plant that was a bit larger than some others, and he stuck down a switch he'd cut at the edge of the field. "There! That's yours; now I'll pick one."

He stuck down another switch, hardly bothering to make a choice, and we went to the house. It was the Fourth of July when I came next to visit Gramp, and as we started supper he said, "Whyn't you run down in the field and see if maybe your tomato plant has a ripe one?" Fourth of July is early for ripe tomatoes in Maine, and as I expected, my plant with its little switch had only green fruit. I naturally went to look at his plant, and it bore six fully ripened tomatoes!

There are tricks to making things grow. Gramp had brought two good-sized stones from a wall and had laid one close to each side of his special plant. He had noticed long ago that even in dry times, a rock will stay moist on its underside. All day his rocks drew the kindly sun to send his tomato plant along, and each night, as they cooled, water condensed to give his plant a drink. We had tomatoes for supper on the Fourth of July.

Gramp was a good cook and on our trips to the woodlot he would bake biscuits in a pail, and grill pork chops, and boil strong tea, and tell me stories of foraging in the army. But his field and barn work made him lazy in his kitchen, and as everybody in the family said many times, he didn't eat right. When I would come, he would suggest various things he'd like, and I had carte blanche to operate the stove. He loved custard pie, and I soon knew how to turn out two and three at a time so they didn't whey. Learning to cook on a farm, with a hungry customer, was a pleasant lesson. Crates of eggs stood in the back entry waiting for the weekly buyer. Gramp was never a dairy farmer, but he always had a fresh cow. I would chase off the various calves she was supporting and we'd have milk and cream. Every meal was a feast. And always his stories — things that happened in the war, family legends, local history.

How he "started" the Battle of Gettysburg. He was on a detail to guard some Rebel prisoners until they could be questioned, and as it was a hot day they put the prisoners on honor and everybody went swimming in this little pond. One of the prisoners started to escape, so Gramp ran for his musket and took a shot at him. He missed, but the noise of the gun alerted both Union and Rebel armies, and everybody began to shoot. That's how the battle began. I had a letter about that from a "historian," and he said it couldn't be true because there was no pond in that vicinity.

Oh, pshaw! It would be a poor Maine author who would believe a historian before he would his own grandfather!

Gramp and I were sitting on his piazza one pleasant Sunday afternoon, and an empty pickup truck equipped to haul live animals came into the dooryard. The man said he was a cattle buyer and had a meat route, and he wondered if Grandfather might have a small bull or steer he could buy.

"I think I have just what you want," said Grandfather. "But it's Sunday, and I don't do business on the Lord's Day. Besides he's up in the pasture, and it's getting late. Why don't you come back in the morning?"

The man promised to return and drove away. As soon as he was out of sight, Grandfather went to the barn, released a two-year bull from his stall, and drove him up the lane into the pasture. When the man came the next morning, we walked up to the pasture, and this bull was standing as advertised.

The man liked the looks of him, they dickered, and the man bought him. I drove him back down the lane, past the barn, and we prodded him into the truck. When the man was gone, Grandfather said to me, "Never sell a bull in the barn. He always looks bigger'n he is when he's pawing a knoll in the pasture."

When I got older Grandfather said he hoped I'd go to "Boardin'" College. (It was the local way to pronounce *Bowdoin*.) He had a special reason: the farm had been bought in the beginning from the same family from which the college took its name, and among his papers he had the first deed, signed by James and Sarah Bowdoin. Gramp always encouraged me to study astronomy if I went to "Boardin'." When I did indeed go to Bowdoin, I soon discovered that astronomy is a bad case of mathematics and that my interest ran otherwise. In Grandfather's lifetime, I never understood his insistence on astronomy.

He died while I was still in college, and I afterwards bought the farm from his estate. A few years later I came there to live and raise my family, and in a burst of comprehension I knew why he had insisted on astronomy. I stepped out one evening into the dooryard for a simple physical purpose, just as my grandfather had done thousands of times, and I looked up to see the night sky as he had seen it from boyhood. There is no place in the world where the stars are so close as on Lisbon Ridge. In summer they blink at arm's length in a soft sky, and in winter one can reach and cut his finger on their crisp edges. To Grandfather, astronomy was stars. He never knew much about them and hoped I might. I never see a star in the sky but I'm reminded of Gramp — and custard pies and bulls in pasture and historians who worship the truth and ripe tomatoes and . . .

27

M Y FATHER did not attend church with pious fidelity, although he was not spiritually opposed to the habit. If his job came right and he was available, he would go to please Mother — as we all did. But after he retired from the postal service the parish elected him treasurer in a rare demonstration of good sense, and after that you couldn't keep him away. His interest was fiscal. The tired little church had its week-by-week money problems, and Dad felt it was his treasurer's duty to be concerned. So he attended faithfully, enduring the platitudes of the morning worship, and waited patiently for the benediction. As the minister moved toward the front door to shake hands with the parishioners, Dad would bound from his pew and race forward to count the collection.

One Easter Sunday the whole family came together to escort Mother and Dad to church. While Dad was shaving, which he always did at a mirror in the kitchen, he kept jawing about this miserable old fool who had lately been "given a call" and was preaching at our church. Dad never understood why the pulpit committee had been attracted to the preacher. "Talk, talk, talk, talk," said Dad, "and says nothing."

Dad said, "He's so poor a harelip would improve him."

He said, "Worst thing is, he don't know when to quit."

He said, "If I could trust the deacons to count the cash, I wouldn't go."

We went to church, and soon after the minister commenced I could see that my father had described the parson with some accuracy. He was pretty bad. And he began missing excellent opportunities to stop. But he kept on going. At last he shuffled the pages of his sermon at length, hesitated, and said, "and in conclusion . . ."

We heard our father sigh and mutter, "Thank God!"

Somebody in the pew ahead heard him and said, "Aaa*MEN!*"

Which was instructive. There comes a time to stop.

Acknowledgments

This whole book of reminiscences seems to be an acknowledgment. I am greatly indebted. But it is disconcerting to observe in the late afternoon that things written in the bright morning have been in the public domain for years. I'm fairly sure the story of the two boys playing woodchuck appeared in the Boston Sunday *Post* around 1932 or 1933; the grand old *Post* ceased publication in the 1950s. With the snows of yesteryear, too, are *Collier's* and the old *SatEvePost*. So who would I thank here? "Faithful to the End" and "A Study of . . . Horn Elevation" appear herein basically intact, and are credited on the copyright page. All other material reappearing here (such as R. P. T. Coffin's whale, Del Bates's piano concert, and the histrionic triumph of Billy Edwards) has been refurbished in trifling or major ways.